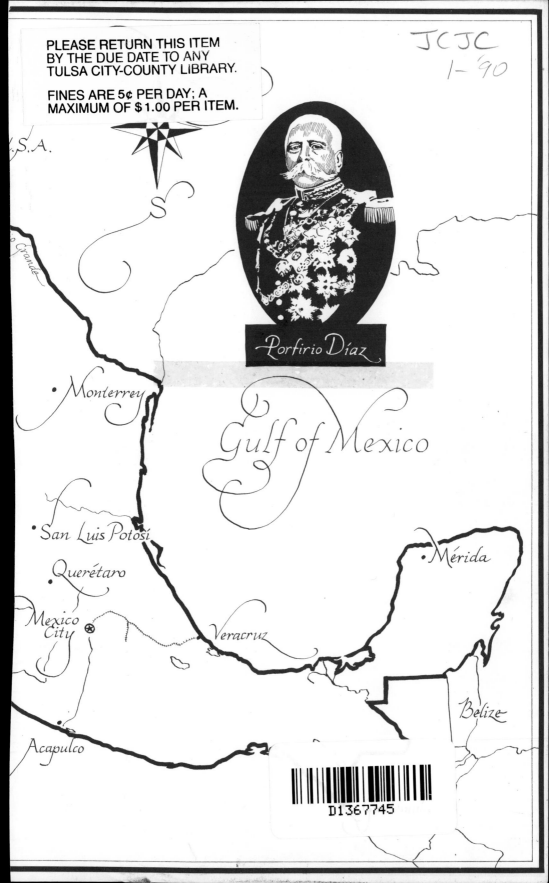

JCJC
1-'90

Porfirio Díaz

U.S.A.

Río Grande

Monterrey

Gulf of Mexico

San Luis Potosí

Querétaro

Mérida

Mexico
City

Veracruz

Acapulco

Belize

El Güero

Elizabeth Borton de Treviño

El Güero

A TRUE ADVENTURE STORY
PICTURES BY LESLIE W. BOWMAN
FARRAR · STRAUS · GIROUX
NEW YORK

To Daniel, Elizabeth, and Leo
E.B.T.

To my parents, Lee and Dick
L.W.B.

HISTORICAL NOTE

Porfirio Díaz was a Mexican army officer who had fought against the French usurpers and the imposed monarchy of Maximilian in 1864, until the French were defeated and expelled from Mexico. He became a popular hero, and enjoyed the taste of power.

In 1876 Díaz turned against the elected Mexican president, Lerdo de Tejada, and, defeating him, seized the presidency. He then began a strong dictatorship which lasted over thirty-five years. The Mexican Revolution of 1910 finally deposed him.

Fearing the wrath of Díaz, Lerdo de Tejada fled to the United States, and with him went many of his followers. But one who remained at his post in Mexico, still loyal to Lerdo, was Judge Cayetano Treviño, the Judge of this story.

In those days, transportation was extremely difficult. There was no railway to the border of the United States, only to Veracruz, on the coast of Mexico. The Pacific port was Acapulco, reached by rough highway. All the roads were poor, almost impassable, and infested with bandits. From Acapulco a few steamers operated along the Pacific Coast, carrying cargo and sometimes a few passengers.

E.B.T.

El Güero

PROLOGUE

Judge Cayetano Treviño had been summoned to the office of Mexico's new president, General Porfirio Díaz. Still loyal to the duly elected president, Lerdo de Tejada, who had been exiled, Judge Treviño awaited arrest, because the dictator Díaz was severe and all-powerful. When the soldiers of the presidency came for him, Judge Treviño left his family weeping and praying, but he mounted his horse calmly and accepted the police escort to the president's office. He fully expected to be sentenced to prison or to death.

He entered President Díaz's office with dignity.

General Díaz, an Indian from the state of Oaxaca, was strong, intelligent, canny, and practical. He was wearing full military uniform.

"You were a Lerdo man," he began, without preamble.

"I was, and I am," answered the Judge. After the short silence that followed, he continued courageously, "I am a man of law, Your Excellency. I believe that a system of law governing the conduct of the public is the finest invention of the human mind. Lerdo was properly and fairly elected, and I consider him to be the rightful president."

He then stood awaiting the sentence that President Díaz

might impose. It was possible that Díaz would consider the Judge's words treason.

"Well, we admire the same things," commented General Díaz thoughtfully. "You follow the letter of the law. I believe in making it work. I, too, believe in justice, and as a soldier I am ready to fight for it. This country is in chaos; Lerdo could not control it. There are bandits on all the highways; a man cannot be safe on the streets without a bodyguard. Something had to be done, and I have done it.

"You, Judge Treviño, would have criminals brought to court, tried, and sentenced. I tell you we haven't courts enough or prisons enough or time enough to carry out the process of law you stand for. I say, fast justice; shoot criminals in the act. We must have order."

Judge Treviño made no answer.

"I do not kill my enemies," said General Díaz. "Only the enemies of the public. You are a judge, and you shall continue as one. But not here. I am assigning you to a small border town where a court must be established. You will depart at once for Ensenada, in Baja California. You will pick up your orders from my clerk."

Judge Treviño stood as if stunned.

General Díaz turned back to his papers and made a gesture of finality. "Next appointment," he snapped.

Judge Treviño stumbled from the room. Outside, he found his horse, still tethered in the courtyard, mounted it and began the ride home.

1

My name is Porfirio, but nobody ever calls me by my name.
It is because most people in this country have dark eyes
and dark hair, while my eyes are green and my hair is
yellow. It is for this reason that everyone calls me El Güero,
or the Blond One. My little sister, María, is called Maruca.
I call my Aunt Victoria Tía Vicky, and my mother Mamacita. Everyone in Mexico has a nickname, or a short,
affectionate form of his name. Only my father, the Judge,
who is so dignified and taciturn, is called by his name,
Cayetano, and then only by Mamacita and Tía Vicky. I
have been told to call him Papá, though the other children
I know call their fathers Papacito, dear little father.

On the day our great adventure began, I was at school,
as usual. We were studying geography and drawing on a

map the boundaries of Mexico. I had no idea that in a few days my whole family would be traveling toward the northern border.

I was called out of class and taken hurriedly home by our *caballerango*, our stable boy, Epifanío. I sat up front in the carriage with him.

"What is the matter? What has happened?" I asked, and I was worried because my Mamacita was delicate, and often had terrible nervous headaches.

"Your father the Judge has come home and has told us to pack up your family to leave," replied Epifanío, as he gave the horses a flick with his whip.

"To leave? To leave the city?"

"To leave the region," he answered.

At that I was silent, as we clop-clopped along, until we had come to our own big *zaguán*, our carriage gate, and Epifanío turned into the driveway.

I found Mamacita in tears, and Tía Vicky with her. My father was home. He told me quickly that we must choose a few things we loved—only three—and pack two sets of clothes. We were going away, to a strange part of Mexico, and we could not carry much baggage with us. He had been exiled by the president, and we must leave within two days.

At first I enjoyed the excitement. Everyone was running about. Mamacita and Tía Vicky were packing up bedding and kitchen things, and crying all the time, and old friends of my father came visiting. But then I learned that I had to leave my pony and my dog behind, and Maruca had to leave her cat Michi-Fu, who was going to have kittens. So she was crying, too. Finally our cook, who was also in tears, said she would take my dog and Michi-Fu, and Papá sold our horses and my pony to a friend who would take good care of them. I hated to say goodbye to my pets; they were like people to me, and I loved them. I hated to leave the servants, too.

Papá explained that we were to be taken over the highway to Acapulco by Don Leandro, an experienced leader of caravans, who supplied his own horses and mules. This journey would take many days, and then we were to embark on a steamer to carry us miles to the north, to Ensenada in Baja California.

We set out while it was still dark. Maruca was asleep, in the little riding chair they had made for her, slung across a mule's back. There was one for me, too. Mamacita and Tía Vicky rode mules, and Papá was mounted on a horse. He rode up in front with Don Leandro, a tall, thin man with a long mustache. Then came the baggage mules, and Don Leandro's men, who rode alongside us and in the rear, to keep watch that all was well, and to defend us.

I was wide awake. I didn't want to miss anything, for this was the first Big Adventure of my life.

Everything that happened was unusual and strange. For example, when we stopped for breakfast, it was one I had never tasted before. The men had made coffee over a fire, and they gave us *tlacoyos*, thick cakes of blue corn stuffed with beans. They tasted wonderful to me, and I loved the coffee, black and strong and sweetened with dark sugar. At home, I had always breakfasted on sweet buns and hot chocolate. But this was only the beginning. Sometimes the men rode ahead and shot quail and broiled them over the fire, and once Don Leandro even shot a deer and we feasted on venison.

Along the way were travelers' huts here and there, small stone shelters in which the family slept on blankets on the floor, all five of us, while the men slept by a fire outside, one always keeping watch. In the morning we washed in streams, and started out early on the road again.

About three days into our journey, when we had halted under the shade of some trees to rest the animals, we saw a cloud of dust on the road ahead. It was early in the afternoon. Instantly Don Leandro ordered the men to form the beasts into a circle and he told us, Papá and Mamacita and Tía Vicky and Maruca and me, to get inside the circle and stay there.

"There are many bandits on this road, Judge Treviño," explained Don Leandro. "Very few caravans get through without being robbed."

My father saw that the men had taken out their rifles, and that Don Leandro had a pistol.

"No shooting," ordered my father. "If we are accosted and they are hostile, we will parley."

We waited. A group of masked men came toward us, pulling up their great horses a little way from us. There was a silence; I could hear the creaking of the leather saddles, and the breathing of the horses. Then Tía Vicky let out a terrified sob.

The leader dismounted, dropped his mask, and cried, "Judge Treviño!"

My father made no answer, and the bandit leader went

on, "I know you, Judge. You sent me to prison five years ago. I was tried for murder in your court. I am Victor Cobián."

"I remember you now," said my father. "And today you assault innocent travelers on the highway!"

"They call me El Chato now," the man went on. "Yes, we ride the highway. We have to eat. And nobody would give us work, knowing we had been in prison."

"What are you going to do with us?" I asked El Chato. I was afraid that he was very angry at my father for having sent him to prison.

"Why, nothing, *joven*, young man. We are going to protect you. How far are you traveling, Judge?"

"To Acapulco."

"We, my men and I, will watch over you all the way. I am grateful to you, for you believed me when I told you that I had killed in defense of my home. No one else believed me. They would have had me shot at once. But you were merciful. You gave me a short prison sentence."

"Señor Cobián," said my father with dignity, "I cannot accept favors from a bandit. I am a man of the law."

"Well, in this case, you can't help yourself" was the answer. "We will protect you whether you like it or not! I am known on these roads and the other bands respect me. You will be safe."

"Cayetano," whispered my mother, "thank him."

At her words, my father smiled and bowed slightly. "Since we are fellow travelers," he said, "you must accept our hospitality. Please have some coffee."

At first the road rose slowly upward into the mountains. It grew colder and we were glad of the little travelers' shelters. Later, when we dropped down into a lower and warmer country, we often slept in hammocks that the men slung between the trees, first tying bunches of thorns into the ropes. The thorns were to keep scorpions from walking down from the trees and onto us while we slept. The hot country was famous for these small reddish insects, whose sting could be mortal. Once we even found a large dark blue scorpion, almost four times as large as the others. When Don Leandro squashed it, it gave off a smell like vinegar.

As soon as we got to the hot plains, Don Leandro stopped at a village and bought white cotton cloth, which he cut up and fashioned into a sort of cape for each of us, with a hole for the head. We were to wear these over our clothes so that we could see leeches as they fell down on us from the trees. We were also given a strong flexible branch with which to brush them off. There were snakes, too; we had to be vigilant all the time.

There were so many things to learn! So much that was new and strange.

Once in a while, we would come to a village where we could bathe and sleep in beds. When we did, Tía Vicky, who had never done any housework in her life, begged soap from the villagers and set to washing everybody's clothes. She had stopped crying about a week into the journey, and seemed to be enjoying herself. She became very bossy with everybody. I heard my mother complain softly to my father about her, but he answered, "Good, Juanita. Let her be. A weeping woman is no help on a dangerous journey, but a bossy one can be useful." Later on, I was to see the reason for his words.

Maruca fell sick with a fever. Tía Vicky demanded that we stop in the next town and find a place where she could take care of her. But Don Leandro said, "No, señorita. We must go on. In Acapulco we can buy the white powder, quinine, to cure her; if we stay here, without the medicine, she will die. We are not so far from the port now. In two days' march, we will see the ocean."

Tía Vicky was angry, but she obeyed. She rode beside Maruca, who slept and whimpered in a kind of daze. Tía Vicky had a gourd of water with her and she kept sponging Maruca's forehead with a wet cloth, to cool the fever. And at night she slept close to Maruca to keep her warm, because at night she trembled with cold. We were all silent and worried, and Mamacita clamped her lips shut and tried not to cry.

"My little angel is so delicate," I heard her say. "I will lose her on this horrible journey."

"Have faith. Be strong, my love," Papá whispered, putting his arms around her.

I was very sad for Maruca and also for Mamacita. They were suffering, but most of all, I felt sorry for my father, who had brought us on this adventure. I knew that he felt guilty and unhappy to be the cause of so much trouble.

My father was almost a stranger to me, because he had always gone to his office before I had awakened and had breakfast, and at night he had been tired, and we children had been ordered to be quiet, and not noisy and troublesome. We had our supper an hour before Mamacita and Papá had theirs; we kissed his hand and said good night, and he placed his hand on our heads and blessed us, but we never stayed to talk and tell him about our days. On Sundays he and Mamacita often went to dine in the homes of other judges and lawyers, or sometimes Papá sat in his library in our house, studying his cases.

But now, on the journey, we were close to him all day, and often, when we stopped to rest the animals, he dropped his arm across my shoulders and told me about when he was a boy and how later he studied in Monterrey. There he had written poetry and had declaimed it before large audiences.

"I have it written down somewhere," he told me, "but I have forgotten it all."

We even laughed together, as he remembered some anecdotes of the time when he was a young man learning the law.

It was wonderful now to hear him shout, first thing every morning, "Where is El Güero? Where is my son?"

Don Leandro hurried us along, and as he had promised, by evening of the second day he halted us on a high part of the road and told us to look. Acapulco! And there, below it, was the ocean. I had never seen the ocean, and I did not expect it to be so large. It was like a piece of blue silk, stretched out as far as the eye could see. We came down from the hill and went closer and at last we could take in the sharp salty smell and hear the ocean breathing.

There was a splendid white ship riding on the waters of the bay and it was due to sail the next day for the north. I asked if we would travel on it, but Papá said no, we must wait and get Maruca well before we ventured any farther.

We took rooms in a simple hotel and Papá found a pharmacist who sold him the quinine powder, made from a tree in Peru.

Chato and his men had left us two days before, and Don Leandro was busy arranging to accompany other travelers back to Mexico City. My father had given each of the men in both bands, Don Leandro's and Chato's, a present of money. He had gold pieces hidden in a *víbora*, a flexible woven belt, inside his clothes.

While Maruca got better, I was free to roam the beach and play in the waves that came hurling in, dashing themselves into foam on the sand.

After about a week, Maruca could walk around again, and she began to eat. Papá bought more of the quinine to

take with us, and told us that now he would go and buy
passage for us all on the first ship going north to San Diego
in California. We needed to go there to get our supplies.

The ship turned out to be a Portuguese freighter called
Esperança. My father met with the captain, a man named
Silva—who didn't look much like a captain to me. I
thought he should have been in uniform, with a cap and
perhaps a sword. He was a short, dark, fat man wearing
greasy trousers and shirt, and with a red bandana on his
head. He demanded the passage money in gold and said
he was sailing the next day. We all went aboard with our
baggage and fitted ourselves into the small rooms, with
their narrow wooden bunk beds built into the wall.

We slid out of the bay and into the great ocean just at
sunset. The ship had a strange smell and it moved along
easily, so silently, we thought, after our many days riding
to the sound of horses' and mules' hooves beating against
the road. But once out at sea, there came the steady sound
of an engine, and the ship began to sway in the water, up
and down, and also from side to side.

At this unaccustomed motion, Mamacita and Tía Vicky
and Maruca all became very sick and had to lie on their
wooden bunks, and couldn't eat. But Papá and I did not
mind and we walked the decks and explored the ship. We
went down into the lower part of the ship and watched
almost naked men throwing shovelfuls of coal into a great
furnace, which made the steam to carry us forward. When
there was a good stiff breeze, the captain hoisted sails,
stilled the engines, and then we skimmed over the water
without a sound.

Watching from the rail of the deck, we saw a school of flying fish one day, almost like birds, with the sun shining on them, so that they seemed to be silver, and another day we saw dolphins leaping and playing in the sea around us. We were never so far out at sea that we could not see the distant shore, a smudge of blue and tan against the sky.

What we did not like was the food, very heavy and salty, but Papá said to eat it up, as we were not carrying any food of our own, and we had to keep up our strength.

"We will need all our strength, Güero," he told me, "to take care of the women. They are all seasick, and will be weak and wobbly when we get off the ship in San Diego."

"When will that be?"

"Captain Silva says in about ten days."

But we did not disembark in San Diego.

A few days later, when we saw land rather close, the ship came in slowly and carefully until we could make out rocks and a beach and, in the distance, a little white building.

"Are we stopping here for supplies?" my father asked Captain Silva.

"For water. And to put you and your family off" was the reply.

"But you can't! I have paid in gold for our passage all the way to San Diego."

"I am obliged to change course," answered the captain. "You can order me arrested next time I dock at Acapulco," he continued, disrespectfully. "You and your luggage are being put off here. I will carry you no farther. We are making for some islands, and I have just enough food for my crew and me. None for you. So get ready. The men will take you ashore in rowboats."

I could see that Papá was furiously angry. He turned quite white and a little pulse beat in his cheek as he clamped his jaws together. But even I could tell that there was nothing we could do.

Mamacita and Tía Vicky and Maruca could hardly walk the few steps on the deck, and the crewmen were kind and carried them into the rowboats. As we got to the beach, the boats grated against the sand, and we jumped out, my father and I getting wet to the knees. The crewmen carried the women up a little way. Then they made several journeys carrying buckets to a small spring where fresh water bubbled up, and went back to the ship. One more trip and they brought our luggage and threw it down.

I went with Papá up a long, sloping hillside to the white building we had seen perched on the top. It looked clean and inviting in the sunshine. I pushed open the door; it was empty.

Mamacita and Tía Vicky had come toiling up the slope, and when Mamacita saw that we were alone in the empty place, she sank down on the porch and began to cry.

"Cayetano, what are we going to do?" she asked my father, her eyes streaming.

"We will make the best of it. Somehow," answered Papá. "Anyhow," he went on, "be grateful that we are all alive. That pirate could have murdered us all and thrown us into the ocean. Who would have known?"

He was silent then, and went looking about, and seemed to be calculating.

"We will sleep in here," he said. "Güero and I will bring the baggage up, and we can make beds with blankets and coats. Fortunately, it isn't cold. No doubt this is a mission, used occasionally. It has been well cared for, though it is empty. Perhaps the missionaries will arrive in a few days. And there is fresh water near. That is a mercy."

"But what will we eat?" asked Tía Vicky, sobbing.

"The sea is full of fish," I said to her. "We will eat fish, and Papá and I will catch them!"

That first night was eerie, because we were so alone and there were sounds in this strange land that we had never heard before. Some animal howled far away, and then came nearer, and then went away again. The wind rose and made a sad sound and the waves crashed louder and louder on the beach until it seemed to me that they would come and drown us. I got up and went out on the porch to look, but the waves were still a good distance away.

In the morning, in bright sunshine, Papá and I explored.

The place was desert country, very dry and barren. There were a few trees in clumps around another small spring, but many thorny bushes everywhere.

"The thornbushes will do for our firewood," said Papá. "I have a strong, broad-bladed knife with me, to cut them, and matches. But matches can be used up. I think we must keep a fire going day and night, and never let it go out. And we can use it to signal passing ships."

"Papá, I can take branches from the trees to make fishing poles, and the ropes that bound the luggage can be our lines. I will fish!"

"Excellent, Güero. We will manage. Somehow."

I noticed that he had said "Somehow" several times. Perhaps it was wise. Because everything we did, we did "somehow."

Mamacita unpacked her household things, and we went every morning to the spring to fill her pots and pans and pitchers, and bring the water back to the house.

"However, we must conserve this," said Papá. "Springs sometimes retreat back into the earth. We will not use the water for washing. We will wash in the sea."

"But I can't wash clothes in salt water," cried Tía Vicky. "The soap won't make suds."

"Then we will wear our clothes dirty," said Papá. And I thought he hid a little smile, for Tía Vicky was always so concerned about her appearance; she took great care of her hair and her complexion, and even on our long journey on muleback, she had been careful of her skirts and her shoes, and had worn a shade hat.

It was a hard time.

Even fishing wasn't easy. There was no rock or promontory over the water so that we could drop our line into deep water. We had to fish in the surf, standing in the second line of waves, with trousers rolled up above the knees, our feet bare. Sometimes the waves were rough and tumbled me, but my clothes dried quickly enough, for the sun was hot. After a while we got the hang of casting and were able to catch plenty of small flat fish, which Papá gutted and scaled with his knife. Tía Vicky had to tend the fire, and she learned to fry the little fish just right, and for a few days they tasted delicious. But soon we got awfully tired of them.

Papá's feet and legs were sunburned and painful; in fact, we both were sunburned and peeling. Tía Vicky had scissors and thread and cloth in her baggage and she made sunbonnets for Mamacita, Maruca, and herself, which protected them.

One day there was a sudden storm, with heavy rain which did not soak into the dry ground but ran off it. We put out every vessel Mamacita had and caught all the rainwater we could, and it was quite a lot.

Papá told Tía Vicky she could have some to wash with, but she shook her head. She went and burrowed in her boxes and came back with a package, which she handed to him.

"I am tired of fish," she said. "Everybody is. Here is my rice, which I was saving to grind up for face powder. Let us cook it in the rainwater."

Papá thanked her gravely and said, "We will use a little seawater with it, for salty flavor, and save all the rainwater we can."

That simple rice, boiled over the fire, tasted like heaven to us. I looked around at us all as we sat eating it. Mamacita was thin and her hair was all tumbled down, as she had lost most of her hairpins, one by one. But it was curly and didn't look bad. Tía Vicky looked dreamy as she ate. All her ideas for beautification had given way; her clothes were soiled and she had gathered her hair into braids. She was even eating her face-powder rice! Papá looked much older, for in his effort to conserve water, he did not shave, and his beard had silver in it. He had always worn a mustache, but a stylish one, with the ends turned up and stiffened with wax. Now his mustache was bushy, and his hair was growing long and hung over his collar.

But Maruca looked better than ever. She had gained some weight, and from running in the sun and bathing in the sea, she seemed to have recovered her lost health. I saw Mamacita watching her, with satisfaction and joy in her face. Maruca was always a worry.

For some reason I seemed to be growing taller fast; my shirts were all tight and the sleeves too short, and my trousers were also too short. Even my shoes seemed small. But I didn't care, because I went mostly barefoot, anyhow.

Papá and I took turns tending the fire at night. It was getting harder and harder to find enough bushes to burn, and we had to range farther for them. Several times we saw ships go by, and we frantically signaled with the smoke from our fire, but they never stopped or paid any attention to us.

Then one day, when we had lost the spirit of adventure and were just enduring and trying to keep alive, a boat came nearer and nearer. It seemed to be heading for us, and my father ran out and waved his shirt and shouted, and to our joy, the boat came in, and a man stood up on the deck and shouted back at us. It was not a large vessel and did not carry many men. They put down an anchor and lowered a rowboat, and two men began bringing it to shore. As they grated on the sand and beached, an agile little man in a long black robe tied with a piece of rope around his waist jumped out. After him the second man got out, and they pulled the rowboat up out of reach of the waves. The second man was short and brawny and he had thick red whiskers. He came smiling toward us.

"Welcome, welcome!" cried my father. "You can't know how welcome you are!"

Tía Vicky and Mamacita came running down from the house. They took the hand of the man in black and kissed it, so I knew he must be a priest.

"I am Padre José, of this mission," he explained. "And this is Captain Forker, who brought me and my supplies. How long have you been here at Cabo San Lucas?"

"I reckon it to be about a month," my father told him. "We were forcibly put off here, after having bought passage to San Diego."

"Well, I can take you to San Diego," said Captain Forker, "though you may not be very comfortable in my small boat."

"We are five," explained Papá, as Maruca came rushing toward us from the little mission cottage, where she had been asleep.

"We could manage. We could manage," cried Captain Forker, and I could see that Tía Vicky and Mamacita were of a mind to kiss his hand too, they were so relieved and happy to be rescued at last.

There were two sailors on Captain Forker's boat, and they made trips back and forth until they had delivered plentiful supplies to Padre José. There were sacks of beans, flour, sugar, coffee, potatoes, oranges, dried meat, and salt, and casks of oil.

That day we had a feast of beans boiled over the fire, meat softened in water and then fried, and oranges; the oranges tasted more wonderful than anything I ever remembered, we were so hungry for something sweet and fresh. We were to go aboard Captain Forker's boat in the evening. Meanwhile, the sailors were filling great water casks at the spring and getting them aboard.

Padre José put pots of beans to boiling, and rolling up his sleeves, he mixed flour and water and began patting out flat tortillas and cooking them over the coals. "See?" he said to me, moving his head slightly, and I looked toward the distant hills. People were coming from them, more and more, getting closer and closer. They were Indians, ragged and hungry.

"They expect me," he explained. "They watch for Captain Forker's boat. When they have seen that you are gone, they will come in close to me. Then I will say Mass for them, and marry them, and baptize the babies. I go up and down this long peninsula, from mission to mission, bringing Our Lord and also food and hope. They are good souls, but very shy."

As twilight fell and we were rowed out to the boat, we saw the Indians crowding in around Padre José. He met them with kisses and blessings.

3

We were two nights and three days on Captain Forker's boat, which was called *Emily*, for his dead wife, he told me. "She used to come with me on every voyage," he said, "and cook for us in that little galley."

The galley was a narrow space, with a tiny stove and a few utensils hanging from hooks above a little sink. To one side was a barrel of water, and a dipper. Water was scarce, and we were each allowed only three dippers a day.

"Mostly, water is what I carry," explained Captain Forker, waving an arm toward the sealed barrels stacked on the deck. He also carried some supplies to the settlements along the coast, but these barrels were all filled with water. "They are heavy, Güero. Just taking you and your family aboard lowers us a bit more in the water. Look.

But no matter. These waters are usually calm. When I smell a storm coming, we put in for land and stay out of the way. That is why we steer so close to shore."

The small boat had a strange movement, from side to side, which made me dizzy at first, but I got used to it.

"You'd make a good sailor, Güero," praised Captain Forker. We became friends. He told me how, once a year, great pods, as he taught me to call them, of gray whales came down from the north and swam along peacefully, blowing streams of water into the air and making strange humming noises to each other.

"I believe they talk to each other," he told me seriously, "but I don't dare tell most people because they will say it is a crazy old sailor's yarn. But I have seen that they seem to answer each other, and the sounds they make change, too, as they go along."

"Why do they come?" I asked.

"They come down from the cold northern waters to have their little ones here, in warm safe bays," he explained. "And if one doesn't bother them, they are kindly beasts, almost tame. But sometimes the whalers come in after them, and I hate to see it, I truly do."

Papá and Mamacita and Tía Vicky just sat and dozed on the floor, with their backs up against the water casks; there were no chairs or anything of the sort on deck. "This is a working vessel," explained the captain.

Maruca and I were free to roam around if we didn't get in the way of the two sailors. Sometimes they worked very hard, for when there was a little breeze, the captain put up sails, to save his fuel.

"I am going to have to stop at Ensenada," he told us. "You had better get off too and look around and see what you are going to need. Then you can buy it in San Diego and bring it back with you when we make the return voyage."

That seemed sensible, and Papá agreed.

"You will have to make careful lists," Papá told Mamacita, "for the house and for personal use, as I doubt if there is much choice in the shops in Ensenada."

Papá was right. When we got off the boat and stepped on the little wharf built out into the bay, we saw that there were no shops, no church. Nothing!

Mamacita didn't say one word, as we stared around at the long beach, the extending plain, the line of hills.

Captain Forker came up. "You'll want to go over to the barracks, to show your papers," he said. "Here comes Captain Alanis, with a detail of men to inspect my boat, as I have foreign registry. And he often gives me a list of produce to bring back from San Diego."

The sun was hot, but Captain Alanis was wearing a tight-fitting uniform and a cap. He was sweating. He was erect, and snapped out orders to his men, who were not at all well dressed, and slouched in dirty trousers and tunics. One of them had a parrot on his shoulder. He told me not to come near his parrot, as it was jealous and loved only himself, and bit people it didn't like.

Papá explained his situation and showed his orders to Captain Alanis, who said, "I will save you a walk to the barracks, Judge Treviño. There are no houses here at all; there is no town. There are a couple of ranches north of here, and Don David Zárate, a miner, has a house over there near the bay. There is nothing else. We have our quarters, which are poor and cramped. I cannot lodge you and your family, or even feed you. We are short on rations ourselves. Mexico City forgets us, much of the time."

"Then what can we do?" cried Mamacita.

"You could find a big spreading tree and live under it for a few months," answered the captain. "We did. Until the Indians come down from the hills. Then you may persuade them to build you a shelter."

Giving instructions to his men, he saluted, and took Captain Forker aside, whereupon they conversed quietly. Then I saw Captain Alanis put some coins and a paper into the old seaman's callused hand. In a small voice Mamacita said, "I don't see any spreading trees."

Overhearing her, Captain Alanis came and said, "There to the left, near the hills, there are some large oaks. That would be the best place. There is a small stream, and it is close to where the Indians come down to camp. I wish you a good voyage."

Saluting again, he walked briskly away, leaving the soldiers to follow with the few stores Captain Forker had brought for him.

We were all very quiet as we waited to get back on the *Emily*.

It wasn't a long way to San Diego. We arrived the next afternoon and my father arranged with Captain Forker for our return trip a week later.

"Meanwhile," Papá told us, "we will go to a hotel where we can all have baths and a good meal, and make our plans."

"Perhaps we ought just to stay here, in San Diego," said Mamacita.

I knew what Papá would answer. And he did.

"I was ordered to set up court in Ensenada," he said. "You may stay here, my dear, if you prefer, with the children and Victoria."

Mamacita drew a long breath. "If you must live under a tree, Cayetano, I will make us a home there. Somehow. And now we will find a church and go and give thanks that we are safely here."

Maruca whimpered, "I don't want to live under a tree!"

Tía Vicky, though, tossed her head. "*Vamos*—Come now! It will be fun! No floors to scrub, no dusting of furniture! Brace up, Maruca. It will be an adventure! You will tell your children about it someday!"

It was a great adventure at first. But it was hard work, too.

We slept on canvas cots, with sheets over our faces because of the flies. My father made Mamacita a stove out of rocks, where she could put on water to boil, and make coffee, and cook our meals. Maruca and I had to bring buckets of water three times a day from the stream.

Some distance away, under another tree, Papá dug a pit, and then set up stakes and draped canvas around; this was our bathroom. He contrived a shower too, with canvas shaped in a tube that we could get into. Someone outside could then pour buckets of water down over the person inside. This was usually my job and we made stone steps that I could climb up, with my bucket.

There wasn't much water in the stream, really only just

enough flowing so that we filled our buckets by letting them lie on their sides in the water. But one of the soldiers told us the stream would be full and noisy after the rains began back in the hills.

Papá could not set up his court, as he thought it impossible to do so in the open, under the tree, so we explored all around, as far as we could walk, until the Indians should arrive.

At last we saw Captain Forker's boat in the bay once more, and he was bringing Padre José with him. He had picked up the priest at a little village halfway between Ensenada and Cabo San Lucas, where we had lived in his mission house. Padre José had done the rest of his journey on foot, and his soutane was all dirty and torn. He needed new sandals, too.

"My Indian people will be coming in now, within a few days," he told us. "Señora Treviño, I will need your help."

"Of course. Tell me what to do," Mamacita answered.

"We must have food ready. Great *casuelas*—clay pots— of beans. I will ask Captain Alanis to have his cook make bread for us . . . plenty of loaves. Captain Alanis is reluctant, but I press him," said Padre José briskly, "and the cook is friendly. I shall also need you to stand godmother to all the children who must be baptized."

"Oh," cried Mamacita. "But they must be taught, learn their religion . . ."

Tía Vicky broke in. "I'll teach them as they grow older. And to read and write, too."

"These are good people," continued Padre José, "but they are wild and do not really like our civilized ways, or life with us. But they are gentle, and for a while some of them will stay with us, and make bricks and build. There are several different tribes, and these are most friendly and helpful. I know their languages and I will ask them. But you must feed them, meanwhile. Then they will go back to their hills and their own customs."

"We have plentiful stores of food," said Papá, "and I can order more. I will need a house for the family, and a room, apart, for a court."

"Fortunately, there is the right clay for adobe bricks," said Padre José. "Look at the jail over by the barracks. They built that."

It was a simple, one-story, low-ceilinged hut, with no windows; the walls seemed to be thick, judging by the depth of the recessed door, which had a small barred opening at the top, to let in air.

The Indians came very soon, moving in small groups, silently, from the hills. They were thin and hungry, dressed in skins, and almost every woman had a baby in her arms. And there were many children.

Padre José was waiting for them, to embrace and bless them, and some of them knelt before him and he put his hands on their foreheads. When they came near where Mamacita was busy with fires and cooking pots, they shied like nervous horses and trembled, as they did whenever a person who was strange to them appeared. Each one took his or her clay bowl of beans, and piece of bread, and went apart, to eat quietly and share with the children.

After all had been fed, Padre José put on a stole and set out a *casuela* filled with water, which he blessed, and then

he began baptizing the infants. The Indians had seen this before, and they formed in lines and passed their babies to him trustingly. After he had wet the little heads, Mamacita took the babies from him and gave them back to the waiting parents.

At one point he turned to Mamacita and said, "They would get tired and bored if I said the whole ritual for each baby, so I will say it at the end, to cover all of them. Tomorrow we will have the marriages. In the same way. The ceremony at the end, to serve for all."

He sighed. "I wonder if it does much good; I am afraid they just think of me as a kind of witch and put up with our faith only to ward off evil. But," he said, "the Holy Spirit must work through the holy words, and so I continue, and pray that all may be saved."

Thus Mamacita became godmother for about eighty infants.

Before Padre José finished, a stout Indian boy, about twelve years old, came up and knelt down at his feet.

"But, Simón," said Padre José, "I remember you. You are already baptized."

"Yes, Padre," the boy answered in slow Spanish. "But bless me. I wish to stay and work for the white people. And learn to read and write. Then I could become a great chief."

"I will bless you," said Padre José, and made the sign of the cross.

"And I will teach you," cried Tía Vicky. "You can stay and help us."

"Where do you live?" asked the boy.

Tía Vicky laughed and pointed. "Under that tree! There is plenty of room!"

"I accept," answered the boy gravely. "I am Simón. Padre put the water on my head and named me. But my real name is Brazo Fuerte. That means Strong Arm. Look! I am very strong!"

He ran to a big stone nearby and lifted it, and then he threw it a few feet away. He stood panting, looking very proud.

"You are certainly strong," said Tía Vicky briskly, "and I shall have to ask you to do many things for me that I am not strong enough to do. Or Maruca. We must build a schoolhouse, for one thing. And a house to live in. And some tables and benches. Can you find me the men who make bricks? And someone who can hew logs and split them and make furniture?"

"Yes. I go" was the answer, and he left at a trot.

"*Ay de mí*," murmured Mamacita. "Now he is running away. How can we get workers, Padre José?"

"Never fear, the boy will come back and bring them" was the reply. "He is already something of a 'great chief,' because he knows some Spanish."

But we didn't see him again for two days and Mamacita was in despair. She and Maruca, who loved babies, were busy with all the little ones, and there was lots of cooking to do for all those people. Padre José lined them up and married some of them, and said special prayers for the ones who had died or were sick.

Then Brazo Fuerte came back, with four stout young men who stood shyly waiting to be greeted. Padre José had explained that the Indians did not like to be touched and avoided handshaking, so my father went to each one and bowed. Brazo Fuerte said, "Come now, and show us the places where you wish us to build. Then we go to gather straw and to make the bricks."

My father chose land near where we lived under our oak, with our pots and pans and crossed sticks on which we had hung clothes, and our canvas cots. About a mile away, where the hills began, and about half a mile down toward the sea, was a pleasant level place, with a few cypress trees standing on it. The cypresses were bent, leaning into the breeze from the sea, but they were sturdy and smelled sweet.

"We will call our place El Ciprés," said Papá, "and in due time I will have it surveyed and begin to see about land titles. That will be one of my first duties in court. I don't expect to have to try any criminal cases, as I presume Captain Alanis takes care of any violence."

But we learned later that Papá was wrong, because there were criminals. Mostly they came down from the United States, because the frontier had not yet been clearly established and because many adventurers thought Baja California was a place that could not be defended and was open to anybody. Filibusters especially came seeking gold. These adventurers harassed the settlers who began to come in from the south when it became known that my father had set up court and was in touch with the Mexican government and confirming land titles.

We came to know the family named Zárate. That is, I came to know David Zárate first. He was a boy about my own age, a strange, silent boy. He came often to where the Indians were making the adobe bricks for us, and he seemed able to talk to them. But he spoke a little Spanish, too.

Some of the adobe bricks were already drying in the sun. There was a pit where the clay was thick and oozy, and this the Indians formed into bricks, with straw from the dry grasses. They had made frames of wood, into which they patted the mixture, and there the bricks took shape.

"Ho! When it rains, they will all melt!" I cried.

David, who had never spoken to me, said, "No. They will dry firm and strong. You will see. My people have known how to do this for many years."

"Your people?" I asked. He was a white boy, like me. Yet he pointed to the Indians and called them his people.

"Yes. I lived with the Indians for a long time," he said, "and I know their language and their ways. I have an Indian name, too. El Coyote. That name was given me because I can run very fast."

"Let's see how fast!" I challenged, and we had a good race down to the beach. He beat me easily.

I told my parents about El Coyote.

"Yes," Papá told me. "Don David Zárate, the boy's father, told me the story. The child was kidnapped when he was an infant. No, not kidnapped exactly, but taken away to the hills by his Indian nurse.

"It seems that Don David is a miner, frequently away looking for gold and silver in the hills, and then he tries to interest the Americans on the other side of the border to invest in his mines. Once when he was gone to the north, his wife took sick and died, and the daughter, a girl of about sixteen, decided to go to San Diego and try to find him. She left, probably on a boat with some fishermen going toward the north, and the Indian nurse, finding herself alone with the boy, simply started out for the hills and her own people, taking the baby with her. The child was brought up with the tribe.

"Somehow the girl located her father and he tried for six or seven years to find the nurse and his son. But the tribes moved about, and never gave white men any information.

"At last he did the only thing he knew to do . . . He offered gold for any information as to the whereabouts of the woman and the boy.

"Eventually he found them. The boy was afraid and reluctant, but the old Indian nurse brought him back, and remained with the family until she died, a year or so ago.

"The boy is an Indian in everything but looks and blood. He must learn to be white."

"I will teach him!" cried Tía Vicky. "And he can teach us. We can learn much from him. All of us."

That is how we three, Brazo Fuerte, El Coyote, and I, became companions, and best friends.

4

Our life became very different, in many ways, after the house, the school, and the court for Papá were built. Our house was simple, merely two rooms. My parents slept in one, and Mamacita set up an altar there, with the image of Our Lord Crucified and the Virgin of Guadalupe. Mamacita had no candles, but we three boys brought her field flowers and beautiful leaves, to adorn her altar. She awaited the return of Padre José, to bless it.

Papá had brought seeds and he started a kitchen garden, which we had to water from buckets brought from the stream.

Months went by and mostly there was little to do. I fished every day. Brazo Fuerte and El Coyote showed me how to find mussels and abalone on the rocks, and I learned to dive down and pry them off with a piece of pipe. They have a great sucking muscle, which is the part you eat, but that muscle is extremely strong, and it was no easy job to collect them.

El Coyote taught me to make snares for birds, and for rabbits, so we ate quite well. Captain Alanis almost never came to us to offer bread, or help of any kind.

"I don't understand him," my father told Mamacita. "He was ordered to cooperate with me."

Tía Vicky put in a word. "Remember, Cayetano," she said, "he has been king here for some time. You disturb his position. Probably he resents it."

We three boys were together most of the time. Brazo Fuerte and El Coyote spoke different languages, so the language we used was Spanish.

Both boys taught me to wriggle through tall grass without making the stalks wave; you could not tell who had passed. And I learned some lore of the plants and trees.

El Coyote's father, Don David, had come to call on us when the school was ready. He had asked if Tía Vicky would teach his son also, when she began classes for us. She eagerly agreed. Señor Zárate owned the house down by the bay, but he was often away, traveling about. And El Coyote lived there only when his father was home. Like Brazo Fuerte, he liked to camp under the trees, or sleep on the beach.

But Tía Vicky struggled with El Coyote and Brazo Fuerte, for often they would avoid class and go away together on some expedition of their own. Whereas I, of course, was forced to do my lessons every day. Maruca had to study with me in Tía Vicky's classes, but she preferred learning to cook, and usually spent afternoons with Mamacita inventing recipes, and collecting wild herbs to make dishes tasty, and tending the little garden, where we grew some onions and carrots and lettuces.

I was startled to see that my book of Mexican history which I had brought with me from home didn't say much about Baja California. I asked my father about it.

"The Spanish explorer Portolá may have put in here for water, or some galleon from the Philippines, set off course by adverse winds, might have waited out a storm in our bay. But the truth is that little is known about Baja California; that is, officially. The frontier is supposed to be guarded but it isn't, and, in fact, nobody knows for sure where it begins.

"And that reminds me," he went on, "I must get a surveyor here to determine what should be the exact center of town, so that we can survey the land and begin to verify land titles. I will go and ask Captain Alanis about this right now."

Just after Papá left, Maruca came to report that some creature had eaten all the baby carrots, just beginning to form under the earth.

"And I saw it!" she cried. "It was so pretty I couldn't bear to hit it. It had a little pink nose, with petals, like a flower."

"Well, that is a gopher," said Tía Vicky. "I don't know what we can do about it. People drown them out, or poison them . . ."

"Oh no!" cried Maruca, who wouldn't even eat chicken

or rabbit, because she had seen them killed and made ready for cooking.

"Well, then," said Tía Vicky.

"Brazo Fuerte said he would take the gopher away by magic," Maruca explained.

What he did, I don't know, because he wouldn't let me watch. He went at night to the vegetable garden and took his flute with him and played strange music there for a while. But, curious as it seems, we saw no more gophers.

"They went to another place" was all he would say.

When Papá came back from his interview with Captain Alanis, he was rather short-tempered. "He bowed and seemed to agree that we must get a surveyor," he told us, "but he didn't write it down, and I didn't hear him give any orders. He acted reluctant. Now, I ask myself, why?"

"Is he afraid his budget won't cover it?" asked Mamacita.

"But I am sure there must be funds for necessary work like surveying!"

"Maybe there are but are not being used properly," put in Tía Vicky.

Papá was very thoughtful, and said no more about the matter until Captain Forker came in with his boat again. Then I overheard him talking with the captain, and he put a letter into his hands, which was to be posted to some other ship going all the way to Acapulco.

"It will be months before you hear," said Captain Forker. "Why not write to the Mexican regional commander in La Paz? I could make sure he gets the letter, myself. And you would get an answer much sooner."

"Let us do as you say," agreed Papá, "though I am asking for money to pay a surveyor, and I don't think La Paz has authority to allocate funds."

"They are military," pointed out Captain Forker, "and they are superiors of Captain Alanis."

They left the whole matter pending, and Papá was soon busy with something far more exciting.

One day a strange boat sailed into the bay and several men, North Americans, came ashore. One was dressed in a uniform; the others were not, but all wore pistols and knives. They proceeded at once to the barracks, to confer with Captain Alanis.

El Coyote and I had seen them disembark, and we went to tell my father about it. He was very happy, thinking it was a surveying crew, and he hurried over to the barracks. I don't know what happened there, but he came home quite dejected.

"I suppose they are not what you hoped for," commented Mamacita.

"They are an unsavory crew," said Papá, "and they mean no good. There are a few Mexicans, but the leader, the one who pretends to be military, is a North American. He offers a scheme to Captain Alanis that is sheer treason. If Alanis will go in with him and his men, they will declare the northern part of our Baja California independent, and then later they will demand to be taken into the United States. The leader's name is Jack Morris, and he claims that he can muster one hundred men, all armed, but he prefers an agreement with Alanis. He promised all sorts of inducements to Alanis—control of all mining rights, control of land tenure, and various bombastic titles. Alanis made him no promises, and pretended that he would think things over. I am sure that Alanis is a man out for his own gain and advancement, but I can't believe that he is a traitor."

"What did you say?"

Papá smiled. "I only listened, but I shall try to get another letter to La Paz, somehow. Captain Forker should be back in about a month."

"Perhaps you should go personally," suggested Tía Vicky.

"And leave you and the family unprotected, in case there is real trouble? No."

I told my friends El Coyote and Brazo Fuerte about all this, and we tried to think of some ways we could defend ourselves, if that became necessary.

Coyote said the thing to do was to go into the hills and live with the Indians until things were calm again. "We can interpret for you," he said. "At least, I know the language of the Cucapas; I lived with them. And Brazo Fuerte is a Pai Pai. He knows where to find them, too."

"I will tell Mamacita and my father. Let us hear what they say."

"But it is spring, and the tribes are always hungry after winter," said Brazo Fuerte. "They will be coming down from the hills soon."

"Then there wouldn't be any point in looking for them," I said. "They wouldn't have any food for us, as they have none for themselves."

*   *   *

The Indians did come in a few days, straggling in, and many of them were sick, especially children and babies. Maruca, so tenderhearted, spent most of every day tending the sickly babies, who cried and would not eat and tossed their heads from side to side.

"What is the matter with them?" I asked Brazo Fuerte.

"*Garrotilla*," he answered. That is the Spanish word meaning croup, but Mamacita's home remedies for this didn't seem to help. We had to dig many graves, and it was such a sad time. Padre José had arrived, and he was weeping and reading burial services often. Brazo Fuerte told me many children had died in the mountains and were buried there.

Then one day, after the Indians had all gone again to their mysterious homes in the hills, Maruca didn't get up. Tía Vicky came to tell Mamacita that Maruca was very hot, and must have cold cloths on her forehead.

Papá, who was always very nervous when any of us fell sick, kept going back and forth to where Maruca lay tossing on her cot.

"My throat is sore," she whispered, "and I can't even swallow."

On the second day, he said to Mamacita, "I am guilty. I was remiss. I didn't find out more about that 'croup' that the Indian children had. It is my fault."

"Why?" asked Mamacita, alarmed. "Why do you say this, Cayetano?"

"The disease is diphtheria," answered my father. "I have seen the gray phlegm spreading in Maruca's throat. We must keep sponging it out, even if she cries and fights to be let alone."

Then began a desperate time. They took turns, Papá, Mamacita, and Tía Vicky, sponging out Maruca's throat, and she cried and resisted at first, and then she became languid and let them do what they would. I was busy keeping a fire going and water boiling, as Papá said everything that touched her had to be boiled.

One morning Papá came rushing to the fire, and he had his razor out, the one he had shaved with, back in Mexico City. In Ensenada, mostly he had let his beard grow and just trimmed it with scissors. Now he thrust the razor into the fire, and then into the boiling water. He went back to where Maruca lay, gasping for breath.

Mamacita and Tía Vicky began to cry, but Papá was fierce with them. "Keep quiet and help me! Hold her! One on each side."

I was watching.

I saw him cut into Maruca's throat, and into the bone inside there. The razor made a ticking noise, and the blood flew. Mamacita wept, her tears pouring out silently. I thought Papá would kill Maruca, and I felt cold all over, but she began to breathe again and seemed to get better.

"Now we will make dressings, around the cut," he ordered, and Tía Vicky helped him. Maruca began to breathe easier and went to sleep. Mamacita sat by her, holding her hand, and Papá and Tía Vicky kept close watch. But toward evening, when the long purple shadows fell, Maruca gave a sort of sigh and then was silent.

"She is dead," said Mamacita. "My little angel is dead,

in this terrible country where you brought us, Cayetano. She is dead!"

Tía Vicky burst into loud sobs, but Mamacita said, "I am sorry, Cayetano. Forgive me. But my heart is broken."

Papá left and went out, walking fast. He started toward one of the tall cypresses. It was a favorite place of his, where he often sat and wrote in his notebooks, and did his letters. I followed him, a little way off, and I saw him throw himself under the tree and put his head down on his arms. His shoulders were shaking and he was crying, ugly, harsh sobs.

I hurried to him and put my arm around him, and I said, "Don't cry, Papacito. Don't cry."

He turned and hid his face against me, and kept on crying, and I held him a long time.

I never called him Papá again, but only Papacito. Dear little Papá. He had done all he could.

5

Mamacita was silent and sad. She had packed up her things and tied them into a roll. She was determined to leave.

"I will take Victoria and Güero with me," she told my father. "I am sorry, Cayetano, but I cannot bear it anymore. I cannot stay in this terrible place where I lost my darling Maruca."

She spoke of returning to Mexico City. But Papacito was silent. When at last he answered her pleading, he said, "I won't stop you, Juanita. I know that you are suffering. But I cannot go. My duty is here."

"How will we go?" asked Tía Vicky.

"The way we came. We will take a ship to Acapulco."

"And the highway?"

"We will take the *diligencia,* the stagecoach."

Her mind was made up. She was only waiting for Captain Forker, to take them in his boat to San Diego, where she would make arrangements for them to travel to Acapulco.

A few days before Captain Forker was expected, Mamacita came to me and said, "Get your things together, Güero. Whatever you wish to take with you."

"But I am not going, Mamacita. I want to stay here with Papacito."

She looked at me, startled, and I went on, "Papacito will be too lonely. He will need me."

"As you please," she said after a while, and she was silent and did not speak to me anymore.

It was dreadful then, as we waited for Captain Forker's boat. I took some flowers to Maruca's grave every day, but Mamacita would not go.

She said, "I have lost her, my baby. I will never see her again. I know that. I am trying to be resigned. But I do not want to see where they have buried her, where she will be forgotten forever in this forgotten place."

Tía Vicky cried and kissed us goodbye several times before she went on board Captain Forker's boat. Mamacita walked on, with her lips pressed together and her eyes dry, and she would not look back. Papacito did not speak. We watched the boat until it disappeared, and then we walked slowly back to our little house. It seemed very empty, even though Brazo Fuerte and El Coyote were there. Brazo Fuerte had brought a rabbit, skinned and ready for the pot, so I put it on to cook. El Coyote made some tortillas from flour and water and cooked them on a pan over the fire, and I boiled water for herb tea, as we were out of coffee. Captain Forker would bring some on his return voyage. He would be back in about a month.

It was a dreary time, because Papacito talked so seldom. He was worried about Captain Alanis. He had gone to the barracks to find him several times, and had come home very preoccupied and serious. We were not happy, and we were not very comfortable. But we managed.

I remember the afternoon that Coyote came running to look for me where I was hoeing the weeds in our vegetable garden. He pointed out a ship turning into our wide bay from the sea.

"It's Captain Forker's boat!" I shouted and we ran down to the wooden pier to wait for it. Papacito came, too, and Brazo Fuerte. The arrival of any boat was an exciting event, and we all loved Captain Forker.

As they came in nearer and nearer, we saw figures on the deck. Two women!

Mamacita and Tía Vicky! I didn't know what to think.

Mamacita stepped down onto the pier and ran and threw herself into Papacito's arms.

She was laughing and crying all at once.

"Oh, Cayetano, forgive me," she cried. "As soon as Ensenada was out of sight, I knew I was wrong. I begged the captain to turn back. Oh, I didn't want to leave you! Forgive me! I must have been crazy!"

"You were, *mi amor*," I heard him answer. "Crazy with grief. Nothing to forgive, my love."

Tía Vicky had great boxes and bundles and packages,

and Captain Forker said she made him run too deep in the water, with all her luggage and purchases.

"Juanita stormed and cried and tried to make Captain Forker turn the boat around and come back, before we had even lost sight of you, on the day we left," Tía Vicky told me, as we started out toward our house. "But he wouldn't. I guess he knew she had to have time to repent. But I took advantage of our stay in San Diego to buy everything we needed. Besides, I spent all the money Juanita had for the trip to Mexico City, so I knew we would be coming back!"

"Poor Mamacita," I said.

"She suffered. It is true, Güero. But she had to learn. I am not married and never will be, but with one's husband, it must be for good times and bad. Besides, I have long known something she had to learn."

"What, Tía Vicky? What thing do you know?"

"That you can't look back," she answered. "The past is gone."

"Shouldn't we have any memories, then?"

"Oh yes. Like pictures in an album. You look at them and remember. But then you put them back and close the book, and get on with the day."

"How did you learn these things, Tía?"

"Oh, old maids know lots of things," she answered, tossing her head. "More than people think they do."

We had a great feast that day. Tía Vicky had brought some cocoa, and we had mugs of it, as our good Mexican chocolate had been used up long ago. She had brought flour and coffee and sugar and all sorts of spices and salt.

Also, she had brought a big box of candy, made in the American style of chocolate and cream. This was wonderful, and we savored pieces from the box for several days.

In the evening, Don David Zárate came and he and Papacito spoke about ordering lumber from a place called Oregon.

Captain Forker said he could not carry it but that they could arrange for a larger cargo vessel to bring it in, and then we could build proper houses.

Time went by. We were all very happy and Mamacita began to sing again, and to sew, and she went every day with flowers to Maruca's grave. Often in the evenings we would all race down to the beach and play in the waves as the sun went down.

Then another boat put into Ensenada and tied up at the pier. It was small, not larger than Captain Forker's, but it carried ten men, among them that American adventurer that we had met before, Jack Morris.

As usual, we had gone to meet the boat and see what it had brought in. As Mr. Morris jumped down onto the pier, he saw Papacito and at once went over to him and stuck out his hand. I saw that my father did not take his hand, but bowed courteously, instead. He said, "What brings you here this time, Mr. Morris?"

"I have brought settlers, Judge. We will take up land and bring in cattle."

As he spoke, other men began leaving the boat. I saw that every man was armed.

"I have had no instructions from my government to verify land titles, or accept foreign settlers," said my father. "May I see your papers and permissions? I presume you bring them from a Mexican consul in California."

Jack Morris smiled. I thought it a nasty smile; it was scornful and triumphant. "We deal with Captain Alanis," he said.

At that moment Captain Alanis appeared, accompanied by an escort of six soldiers.

Papacito greeted him, but Captain Alanis did not answer.

"I think we may have a little trouble with the Judge here," said Morris. "He seems to think we ought to have papers and permissions."

Captain Alanis turned to his soldiers. "Arrest him," he ordered, indicating Papacito. "Put him in the guardhouse until further notice."

"You cannot do this," shouted my father. "I am the civil authority here. On what charge do you arrest me?"

"Insubordination," replied Captain Alanis. "You will be kept quiet and without communication. Incommunicado."

The soldiers fell in, three behind Papacito and three in front, and they began to march back toward the adobe jail, which was a short way from the barracks.

My father made no struggle; I could see that it would be useless and he would just be overcome. He marched away, with dignity, and I followed after.

"Papacito, what do you want me to do?" I cried.

"Tell your mother not to worry," he answered.

But I worried. And so did El Coyote and Brazo Fuerte.

There seemed to be nothing that we could do. Don David Zárate had gone away again, on one of his long journeys, and there was no one else to turn to. Captain Forker? But what could he do, a foreigner? Besides, he was not expected back in port for weeks.

We sat, under one of the cypress trees, looking down at the sea, and over toward where they had slammed Papacito into the little one-room jail. Incommunicado.

"Incommunicado. That means he is not allowed to talk to anybody," I explained to El Coyote.

Brazo Fuerte said, "But he could send a message!"

"I think that would not be allowed either. Anyhow, where would he send a message? To whom?"

"To someone. Some strong friend."

"But how?" I asked. "That jail has no windows. Only a little door, with a small space at the top for air to enter."

"When it is dark, I will go and look and see," promised Brazo Fuerte.

It was very hard telling Mamacita and Tía Vicky what had happened. Mamacita turned white, but Tía Vicky cried, "The brute! Captain Alanis is a brute! I shall write a letter to the authorities in Mexico City!"

"But how would you send it?"

"I guess I would have to wait for Captain Forker and ask him to mail it in San Diego."

"It would take months to reach anyone. If it ever were received," said Mamacita sadly. "And Cayetano is not a partisan of President Díaz, who exiled him, and us, here."

In the silence I suddenly asked, "But what will Papacito eat, there in the jail?"

"I will take him food," said Tía Vicky, and she began to plan what she would cook.

When she had a *casuela* ready, with hot food, I went with her over to the jail. A soldier was leaning against the wall, smoking.

"I have brought the prisoner his food," said Tía Vicky, after bidding the man good evening.

The soldier adjusted the rifle he had slung over his shoulder. "Sorry. He can only have food from the barracks" was his answer.

"I will wait then, to see what they bring him," said Tía Vicky.

"Not permitted. You might speak to the prisoner when we open the door and that is forbidden. He is incommunicado. Go back to your house."

"But what are they going to do to him?" she demanded. "And why is this foreigner here? What are they planning?"

"Señorita, if you know what is good for you, you will go home and keep your mouth shut," answered the soldier. And shrugging, he put his rifle on his shoulder and marched up and down, a few steps each way.

"Wouldn't you like some of this hot food?" asked Tía Vicky in a coaxing voice. She went up close and walked with him, so that he could smell the savory fragrance of the rabbit stew. I saw that she was going to try to make friends, and later beg him to let her see Papacito.

But he shoved her away rudely. "Shut up and go back, or you'll be sorry!" he shouted.

We turned and went toward home. Tía Vicky was angry, her eyes blazing. "I can hardly wait for Captain Forker," she whispered to me. "He will have to help us do something. Get messages out, get help, something! Oh, it is terrible to be a woman and not be able to do more than wheedle and smile and try to coax men to do things for you!"

"But he didn't do anything, the soldier," I pointed out. "Even though you wheedled."

"Just wait," she hissed, stamping her foot. "Just wait. I will think of something! Men out here alone, no women around—no decent food to eat—I will wear him down!"

And she went the next day and the next, but she always came back with flaming cheeks, so angry she was almost unable to speak. But she did find out that they took food to Papá in the jail, just bread and sometimes beans, and they gave him water. Always there was a soldier on guard.

"I hope your father comes back soon," I told El Coyote. "We need him. He will help us."

Brazo Fuerte said, "I think we can speak with Don Cayetano."

"How?"

"Better not tell," he said. "I try, first. And alone. But I must wait."

It was fall, not too cold, but blustery. Grass was high everywhere, almost waist-high. The moon was bright, illuminating everything with a pale light. Brazo Fuerte told me that all things grow sleepy and lose energy when the moon is waning, even people. "That is why," he explained, "you must never plant in a waning moon, but only when the moon is beginning to grow. Then it sends power down to the earth and puts power into the plants and the people.

We never go hunting when the moon is growing," he told me, "only when it is waning, for then the creatures grow weary and careless and we can catch them."

So I knew what he was waiting for.

The days went by, and when the moon began to die in the dark sky, Brazo Fuerte told me that he had spoken to Papacito.

"He wants ink and paper," he said.

I was aghast.

"We can never get those things to him, Brazo Fuerte. The guard . . ."

"You will see. Later."

I was impatient to see how we were to manage, but he would not tell me anymore. That night a breeze ruffled the grass and made the leaves in the trees restless. You could hear the waves hissing and sighing down on the beach, and the night was full of little noises, of branches creaking, and animals moving about.

"Come," said Brazo Fuerte.

"Shall I bring paper and the pen and inkpot?"

"Not yet. I have to get something first."

El Coyote, Brazo Fuerte, and I went toward the jail through the long grass, moving on our stomachs. We made no sound, and scarcely disturbed the grass. Every now and then we stopped to listen and Brazo Fuerte knew a place where he could lift his head and look, without being seen. The guard had brought himself a big rock to sit on, and he was slouched against the door of the jail, seeming to doze.

"You go back a way and then stand up, and go down

toward the sea. If the soldier hears anything, he will think it is you. Throw stones, as if you were playing.''

We parted and he continued along until he was safely in back of the jail. El Coyote and I stood up and skipped stones along toward the beach.

The guard did not move. He seemed to be sound asleep. Then we saw him start awake, raise his head, and then subside again.

El Coyote and I moved very slowly toward the beach, and after a while we strolled back to the house, in the soft dark. Nothing seemed to have happened, and we did not see Brazo Fuerte again that night. But I knew he must be all right. He often stayed out all night, and slept in secret places he knew.

He did not come the next morning until almost noon, and Tía Vicky was cross, because she had wanted him to help her fill and carry the washtub, to set it over a fire outside, so that she could boil our clothes.

"I went into the hills," he told El Coyote and me. He had a handful of reeds, stiff ones, of various sizes. I did not know what he planned to do with them, but he always had a reason for everything he did.

Tía Vicky was storming around, working, trying to distract herself, because Mamacita spent her time on her knees in front of her little altar.

"It is my fault," she kept moaning. "I am repaid for being a coward and leaving. Now they will take away my Cayetano and kill him. I will never see him again. Ay! What have I done, my God, that you should punish me so?"

Tía Vicky went and stood beside Mamacita.

"I used to be the one to cry," she shouted, "but now I will not, and I will not have you crying all day either. Get up from there and come out and help me. And you must go to the barracks and complain and demand and make a big scene. Cry over there! That's where your tears might help."

Mamacita dried her eyes and did what Tía Vicky asked her to, but Captain Alanis would not receive her and the soldiers ordered her away. Only one, a new one, seemed embarrassed and sorry, she said, when she came back. "He's just a boy, about eighteen, and he turned away and wouldn't look at me," she said. "I will go often to see if he is on guard duty. Maybe he will relent and let me speak to Cayetano."

But they changed the guard often and we never knew who was going to stand there, his gun slung over his shoulder, looking out to sea.

6

A few nights later, it began to rain, a soft, whispering rain, and Brazo Fuerte said, "Follow me. And bring the paper and the ink for the Judge to write."

He was worried as soon as he saw the ink bottle. It was too big.

"I have an indelible pencil," I told him. "Would that do?"

I showed him how it worked; if you spit on it, the letters came out in strong violet, like ink.

His dark face glowed with satisfaction, and he showed me what the reeds were for. He rolled the paper tightly around the pencil and slipped it into a reed. These reeds were strong and firm; where they had been cut, the surface was sharp as a knife.

"We know a place where these reeds grow," he told me. "We use them to cut and scrape the animal hides."

"But how?"

"I found a crumbled place between the adobe bricks where I could make a little hole. With a reed like this, I pushed and pushed, until it came out on the other side. Then we could speak through it. That's how I spoke to Don Cayetano."

Brazo Fuerte had gone patiently, night after night, until the reed had pushed through. My father had seen it at once and whispered into it. He had asked for paper and ink.

The plan was that El Coyote and I were to go again toward the beach, singing and throwing stones, and playing.

The guard on duty was one of the older men; he had been smoking. When he saw us, he threw his cigarette away and put his rifle up to his shoulder.

"*Alto!* Halt!" he shouted.

"What do you want?" I yelled back. He pretended to sight along the rifle, but I knew he was just amusing himself, trying to scare us.

"Get away from here, brat!" he shouted. And then I was a little bit frightened, because I saw that there was a bottle of something on the ground beside him, and he had been drinking. This was against the rules, I knew, and I supposed he must have got hold of some of the liquor that Jack Morris had brought along on the boat. We had seen them unloading cases of it. The guard started toward us, muttering and threatening.

El Coyote and I ran toward the beach, and he came after

us, running fast. But just then there was a shot, over at the barracks, and he stopped and turned, and ran back to his place. I supposed he was afraid of being surprised away from his post. What the shot portended, I had no idea. It was followed by shouting and confusion, and I hoped that the men had mutinied and turned against Captain Alanis and Jack Morris.

But after a little time there was a sudden silence, and the guard began walking up and down, stiffly at attention, in front of the jail.

El Coyote and I turned, and hurried home, and then we waited anxiously for Brazo Fuerte. As it grew late, Tía Vicky came out looking for me, and she was nervous and annoyed. El Coyote went off to his sleeping place and I went quietly into the house with her and went to bed, but I was awake for many hours.

In the morning I saw that another ship, like the one that had brought Jack Morris, was anchored in the bay.

Before I could get down to the beach, I saw that men were landing, at least twenty of them. And they were not our Mexican seamen, or soldiers, either. I was apprehensive and I hovered out of sight, some distance away. Then Jack Morris and Captain Alanis came hurrying out of the barracks, and they went down to the shore and seemed to be greeting the men. They all marched over to the barracks. Soldiers came at once to unload the ship and I saw many boxes and crates and heavy, laden sacks. These stores were carried up to the barracks, and at dusk the ship lifted anchor and steamed away.

I stood watching while the ship turned north, until all

the light was gone and the sea and the sky turned dark purple.

Then, to our joy, we heard an unaccustomed sound. The *diligencia*, which came as far down the coast as Ensenada only a couple of times a year. It must be bringing some important person.

El Coyote's father stepped out, and the driver threw down his big bulging valise, and two large roped boxes from the roof. The tired horses were led away to rest and eat before the return journey next day.

We were so happy to see Don David. Especially El Coyote! Don David listened as we poured out our story of what had happened. He promised that he would go to Captain Alanis and protest, first thing in the morning, and make sure Papacito was released.

He said he had seen many little ranch houses going up, and cattle in the fields, and evidences of some families having come to live in the country north of us, not too far from the American border.

"They are good people, and they'll meet requirements," he said. "They will be glad to pay surveying costs and secure legal titles. But there are adventurers ready to fight them, and seize their place, and try to make themselves lords of everything."

I told about the shipload of men that seemed to be friends of Jack Morris, and he grew very angry.

"That man is wanted by the Americans," he said. "He's a criminal, as well as a filibuster and a schemer."

After a silence he said, "I wish our government were not so far away. It will take so long for them to come and defend us, if Alanis is up to any tricks with these criminals."

Tía Vicky told him that we could not send out any messages asking for help, as Captain Alanis was watching us, and that Papacito was incommunicado.

Then I told him about Brazo Fuerte and the long, hollow reed, and he cried out, "If the Judge will write out an Amparo, we could get some justice here. I could show it to Captain Alanis or take it to the authorities in La Paz."

"What is an Amparo?" I asked.

"It is a supremely important document in Mexico," explained Don David. "It guarantees protection for any Mexican citizen against imprisonment or mistreatment by authorities without due process of law. It is treason to flout this document."

"But only Brazo Fuerte is clever enough to creep up to the jail unseen and speak to Papacito. And he hasn't come here all day. Maybe he will come tonight."

Don David and El Coyote stayed to eat with us and we all discussed whether it would do any good for Don David to go to speak with Captain Alanis and plead for us.

"Better not," said Tía Vicky. "They probably would just throw you in jail with Cayetano."

Brazo Fuerte did appear, mysteriously, when the night was very dark and the waves were pounding on the beach with a noise like artillery. Inside the long reed he had a document, written out by my father. Don David read it, in excitement. "An Amparo!" he cried. "Tomorrow morning at first light, I will take it to Captain Alanis and demand the release of the Judge," he promised.

But he did not come back. By afternoon, when we were

all desperate to know what had happened, Tía Vicky went over to the barracks to ask for news. She came back in tears. I had never seen her so dejected.

"It is just as I said it would be. They took away the Amparo and tore it up and threw Don David in jail, too," she reported. "They know we are powerless."

Poor Coyote did not cry, but made his face expressionless.

Mamacita didn't say a word. She turned white and went to kneel before her altar. Coyote folded his arms and stood silent, exactly as Brazo Fuerte did; it was the Indian way.

Tía Vicky grabbed our hoe and went out to work furiously in the garden, and I took a hand spade and worked beside her, weeding. I knew she was trying to figure out some solution, and I was too, but I couldn't think of anything to do. And, besides, I was afraid. What would happen to us all?

Our difficulties increased at once.

The next morning two soldiers came marching over to our house and took up positions in front, just as the guards were doing over at the jail.

"What is the meaning of this?" Tía Vicky demanded.

The soldiers laughed, but one of them did answer her, with reasonable courtesy. "You are under surveillance. We are to guard you and make sure you don't do anything foolish."

"Anything foolish? When you have our menfolk in jail?"

"When they also agree not to do anything foolish, they will be released. But in the meantime you must not try to send out any messages or letters or act against Captain Alanis's authority in any way."

"And if I do?" she demanded angrily, her hands on her hips. "If I get a letter to Mexico somehow?"

"I wouldn't advise it," he answered shortly. And they began marching up and down, very stiff and formal at first, but after a time they relaxed and sat on the ground and smoked and chatted together. When it was full dark, they left.

In the night, when we were sure we were alone, El Coyote, Tía Vicky, and I sat close together over our clay mugs of thin cocoa and talked. Or, rather, we thought out loud. First one of us, then the other. Brazo Fuerte had decided to go back to visit his people. He sometimes did this without warning. And Mamacita would not join in. She had lost heart again, and I began to fear that she would get sick and die of a broken heart.

"Our only hope is Captain Forker," I whispered. "But they won't let us speak with him when he comes in. We are under surveillance."

"Somehow, we must manage it," hissed Tía Vicky, clenching her fists. "Güero, couldn't you go north and intercept him somewhere? Isn't there a little bay or inlet or something, to the north, where you could find him? Where he puts in at a settlement with supplies?"

"There might be. There are no settlements near, but maybe we could signal him somehow. I know he watches the shore with his big glass . . ."

"Well, we must try it," she said. "You and Coyote should start north tomorrow, walking along the coast. Maybe you could find a place where you could hail him. The soldiers should think you are just fishing or looking for clams."

"But when is he due to return?" I asked. "We will have to wait for him—maybe many days . . ."

"I will pack food for you, and you can camp out . . ."

El Coyote's eyes sparkled. It thrilled him, as it did me, to plan an adventure.

"I will go back to Indian dress," he said, "and Güero shall use it, too. Nobody will notice us."

"What is it, this Indian dress?" I asked.

"Just a couple of skins," he told me. "Coyote skins. They keep you warm at night, too. And I know how to find food along the way. But we will need to take water."

"How will we signal?" I asked.

"With the coyote skin" was the answer. "Tie it on a long branch and wave it."

"But if Captain Forker comes at night?"

"Maybe we should make signal fires. And hope they are looking."

"Sailors do keep night watches. Somebody is always awake on deck. Captain Forker told me."

It was a very farfetched and vague plan, but we couldn't think of anything better, so when we had calculated more or less the days when Captain Forker's boat would be returning along the coast, we set out, Coyote and I.

I wore my clothes, very ragged by now anyway, with a coyote skin over my shoulder, and Coyote wore two of them, one in front and one in back. We took wheat tortillas, and a gourd of water, and clay mugs to boil water for tea. Coyote knew all the herbs along the way, and we even had some lump sugar that Tía Vicky had saved from her trip to San Diego.

Mamacita kissed us both and blessed us before we started.

"If a miracle happens and your father is set free, I will come looking for you," she promised.

"And if you are not back here within twenty days, I will come searching for you," added Tía Vicky. "I hope we are doing right, letting you go off alone like this." She had been part of the plan from the beginning, but suddenly she began to feel uncertain. I saw her chin tremble.

"Be strong. Have faith," I told her, as she hugged me.

She straightened her shoulders. "I will. I have to," she said. And she stood outside, her hand on her forehead, shading her eyes, until we were out of sight.

7

Grass was high, and that helped us to leave the house and the barracks without any soldiers seeing us and stopping us. Besides, what could anyone see? Just the heads of two boys, Inditos probably, boys with long hair and skin darkened by the sun. The coyote skins were the same color as the waving grass.

We left about dusk, just after the guards had departed from our house for the barracks. I felt unhappy leaving Mamacita and Tía Vicky alone.

Then I thought, a guard is a guard, and if they are taking care that the women do nothing outside the house but wash and hang up clothes, they would probably guard against an attack by a wildcat or some wandering snake.

We walked until the stars rose high over our heads, and Coyote said it was the hour when the night begins its descent toward dawn. Then we looked about for a place to sleep.

"Better just here in the tall grass," decided Coyote. "Snakes live near the rocks, and anyhow, I wore my snake cord, to protect us."

"How? What is a snake cord?"

"See? Here. I have it wound around my waist. It is a rope woven of spiky fiber. When we lie down, we make a circle around us with this cord. Snakes will not cross it; they will go around. They don't attack, anyway. They only attack when they are scared, or startled. Mostly they run away."

So we lay down, and the grass kept out the little gusts of cold wind, and with our skins over us, we slept well enough.

In the morning we went down to the beach and dug some clams. Coyote made a small fire, with pulled dry grass, enough to boil our water, and we cooked the clams. They made a good breakfast, with a couple of the tortillas that Tía Vicky had made for us.

The beach there was long and flat, studded with boulders, and there seemed to be no settlers anywhere near. We walked on, but by nightfall we had not found any place that Coyote thought safe enough. The land was rocky, with sparse grass and occasional trees.

"We must find a good tree and sleep in it," he said, and studied them, until we came to one with thick branches and heavy leaves. He showed me how, and we each got into a crotch of the branches and hung there, with arms and legs down on each side.

"You'll get used to it," he told me. "It is the safest of all; you won't fall, even asleep. When the wild sheep are moving, the rams are very fierce. They can butt you and knock you down, and stamp on you."

"Is that why you want to sleep in a tree?" I asked. "Did you see any wild sheep?"

"I saw dark clouds of dust, and there are no people living around here. It must be a herd of something. And they are moving south; they will overtake us. But if we stay here, they will pass us by. We will wait, in the morning, until they have gone."

I was tired from the walking and the sun, and I fell asleep, clinging to my branch. I startled awake a time or two, but finally I got used to it, and when it was morning, I felt rested. There were strange sounds, a sort of uneasy rumbling and snapping, with the baaing of sheep in several tones, some lower, some higher, some trembly, as if baby sheep were crying. I saw what Coyote had feared, a large band of sheep, with several huge rams, heavy-horned. They were passing along where we had walked the day before, raising heavy dust. They took their time, pulling up grass to eat and loitering, but the big leaders seemed to be anxious for them to move forward and be on the march. We saw them butting the strays back into line and trying to hurry them along.

"They are frightened," commented Coyote. "Something has scared them. We must wait here a while longer and perhaps we will find out what is after them."

We hadn't long to wait. Two men on horseback, carrying guns, came galloping along. Sheepskins, still bloody, were hanging across the horses behind the saddles.

"They are hunting the sheep, but only for their skins," he told me. "They will turn back north soon; they cannot carry much more."

Later, when we went forward, we found where they had killed the beasts and skinned them, leaving the carcasses for the wild creatures to eat.

"Shall we cover this meat over?" I asked Coyote. "It will draw the mountain lions."

"No. They won't venture down. They have been frightened by the shots. The meat is fresh. We will eat some ourselves and leave the rest for the birds."

We made a fire and roasted some pieces we were able to hack off.

"If we had time, I would cut strips and dry them in the sun, to make jerky. But we can't delay."

After we had eaten, and packed some of the fresh-roasted meat to take with us, we started walking north again. The land began to rise steeply. Looking down toward the sea, we found a place where cliffs surrounded a small cove which seemed to be free of boulders and rocks.

"This is a perfect place!" I cried. "We can signal from up here and we will be seen against the sky when they look up."

"Is there some way down?" asked Coyote, and he himself answered by searching carefully to find a break in the cliffside, or a gulley that we might scramble down to the beach. Coyote found one, half hidden by bushes, but they served for handholds along the steep way down. We returned to the top of the cliff to begin our watch.

"Now, if only they will see us! If only Captain Forker, or one of the sailors, will look up," I said.

We sat down and kept our eyes on the sea. After a while, everything became blurry, and I felt very sleepy.

Coyote noticed and said, "The water and the light make magic! They force you to close your eyes!"

"It hypnotizes me. My father told me about hypnotism. You know what it is?"

"Anyone or anything that forces you to sleep, to yield your will. I know. You must not look all the time at the water. Every few seconds, look away, at something here close by."

We took turns and kept watch for the rest of the day, and then, wound in our coyote skins, we slept there on the clifftop, ready to wake with first light.

Two days went by. It was monotonous and I began to lose hope, to be uncertain and worried. Besides, we were hungry. The tortillas we had brought were gone, we had eaten our meat, and we had only some tea.

"You watch. I will snare something—a bird or a squirrel—and find water. The gulleys mean water has been here, water is near. I must go and find it." Coyote went and I was alone. When he came back, he had a squirrel, skinned and gutted, and we made a fire and roasted bits of it. And he had found some water in a little pool, which evidently filled and spilled over, running down toward the sea, whenever it rained. I was so hungry and so glad to be eating that I forgot to watch, but Coyote kept glancing toward the water.

It was Coyote who suddenly stood up, took off one of his skins, and waved it around over his head.

There it was, Captain Forker's boat! I knew it from the shape, and besides, it was quite near. I could almost see the *Emily* painted on its side.

I waved my coyote skin, too, and was shouting, though of course they couldn't hear us.

"I think they noticed us because of the fire," said Coyote.

Anyway, to my joy, I saw that they had put down a skiff and were rowing toward shore. We started down the cliffside at once, falling and hurtling along in our haste. When I landed on the beach of the little cove, I was all torn and scraped, but I was never so glad to see anyone as I was to see Captain Forker, who had come in the skiff with one sailor.

He grabbed me and gave me a great bear hug, and listened as I told him everything that had happened.

"And so we came to wait for you because you are the only one who can help us free our fathers," I finished.

He was silent, thinking. He looked very unhappy and worried.

Then he said, "But I am a foreigner; I have no rights in Mexico. Captain Alanis wouldn't pay the slightest attention to me. He might take it into his head to jail me, too! He needs the supplies I am bringing in, so he will have to let me tie up at the pier to unload. But I'll wager he won't let me leave my boat. And he'll hustle me away."

I told him I had thought of a plan.

"I haven't the Amparo," I said. "But I am the son of a Judge, and I can tell the authorities what has happened and about the Amparo. They surely would know what to do!"

"But the closest Mexican authorities are all the way around the tip of Baja California and up the other side, on the Bay of Cortés, at La Paz," he answered. "A long way."

"Would you take me?"

"Well, I have to, the way I see it" was his answer. "But what worries me now is how I am going to hide you when I dock at Ensenada, to unload the cargo for Captain Alanis. What if they decide to come aboard, to search my boat? They may have noticed that you are not around."

"I will go back and be seen around the house," offered El Coyote, "and I can say you are sick."

"We'll have to risk it that way," said Captain Forker. "So, you come with me on the *Emily*, Güero. Say goodbye to your friend."

But Coyote never said goodbye, and he was already starting to scramble up the cliffside. We waited until we saw that he had safely reached the top, and then I got into the skiff and we rowed back to the *Emily*.

When we climbed on deck, and the skiff had been tied on alongside, Captain Forker said, "Güero, it is not far to Ensenada now, by sea, so I think we should hold off until tomorrow evening so Coyote can get there. That way we can go in at night, unload in a hurry, and steam out when it's still dark."

I was thirsty, and I remembered the water cask that was

reserved for the captain and his crew, as their drinking water, and I went to get a drink. The water in the cask was about three-quarters down. That was when I got the idea that saved us.

The next day, as night was falling, Captain Forker tied up. Two soldiers were there, waiting for him. Sure enough, they pushed past Captain Forker and began a systematic search. But they didn't think to look into each water cask. And there I was, totally submerged in one, with just my nose and eyes above water, and the cover in place. They stamped around irritably, finally did the unloading, and left. I heard them quarreling on the beach about how to carry the heavy boxes of supplies up to the barracks. I kept still and did not move in the water cask.

Captain Alanis came down and, after some talk, irritably paid Captain Forker for the cargo, signed the papers, and departed. At last, with great thankfulness, I heard the sailors casting off, and we began to slide out of the bay. I heard the boat's engine and felt the gentle heave and surge of the waters outside the bay. Even then, I waited and listened. At last Captain Forker bellowed, "Where in tarnation are you, Güero?"

I climbed out of the water cask, dripping, gooseflesh all over me, my teeth chattering.

"We're rid of them, and away!" he shouted and he grabbed me, all sopping as I was, even my coyote skin, and gave me a great bear hug. "Now you take everything off and curl up on my bunk under the covers and get warm. We'll dry out your gear in the sun tomorrow."

The voyage south was smooth, and I was so happy,

knowing that I was on the way to get help—though Captain Forker warned me we would be at sea, and also delivering and taking on cargo, for many days.

I counted the days, and Captain Forker wrote them down in his log.

It was on the seventh day that he wrote, "Storm coming. Must find a sheltered cove."

"How do you know?" I asked him.

"Just like the Indians who study the skies and the animals and the trees and grasses, I study the skies and the water," he told me. "The water has changed color, haven't you noticed? It isn't blue or green anymore. It is a dirty gray. And it is making a different sound. Listen!"

I listened hard, but I couldn't notice any difference, except that the waves were lifting and cresting into foam, and they seemed to be hurrying. One would rise, and then another right behind it would rise and seem to push it ahead. Then the waves began to grow larger and to make a hissing sound.

"Wind from the southwest," said Captain Forker. "We'll have to make haste."

Things began to change rapidly. The wind seemed to groan, and the water became a yellowish green, very ugly.

"Hurricane," shouted one of the sailors, and they started making everything secure with ropes.

"Go below, Güero. We've got to make for shore," Captain Forker said through gritted teeth, and I could see why he was worried. On the landward side there was no cove, only a long sandy beach, with a few trees not far back. Captain Forker made for the shore, as quickly as they could manage. They got the boat through the shallows and up on the beach, where they tipped it over on its side. They made it fast to the trees, and hurriedly got off a few supplies of food and a tarpaulin, and carried them up beyond the sand, to where the earth began. It was dry desert land, with grass and bushes, but no sign of life anywhere.

"God help us," cried Captain Forker. "I hope we can ride it out without losing our ship. If we had stayed on the water, we would have been pulled over and under and all of us drowned."

He ordered the sailors to dig shallow trenches in the earth, and then we all got into them, about a foot or so below ground level. We pulled the tarpaulin over us, but the wind tore it away and wound it around the trees. Then the rain came. It was heavy, lashing, and cold, and the sky got as dark as if it were already night. The water boiled up around the beached boat and made it rock on the sand. One of the trees the boat was tied to came uprooted and fell against it with a terrible noise. I don't know how long we were there in our trenches, which were filling with water but safe from the wind. Captain Forker told me later it was about four hours.

"We were lucky," he said. "The worst of the hurricane is hitting shore north of us. We got only the edge. Bad enough. I wonder what happened to Ensenada."

But when we went down to examine the boat, we saw that one side had been stove in, from the beating of the waves knocking it against the beach.

"I'll have to drag her up higher, and then flag some passing ship to take me to where I can get lumber and a shipwright to come back with me and mend her. She's not lost. But, Güero . . . I am sorry for you. It is tough. Only be glad we are all alive. No one is missing."

"Tougher for you," I had to say, but my heart was really sinking, and I felt desperate.

Perhaps because of the storm, no ships passed, and we were stranded for a few days. I forget how many. We were able to get some stores out of our beached boat, and there was water still in the sealed casks. Our drenched clothes dried quickly enough. But the waiting and hoping for rescue was disheartening, though Captain Forker said he knew the boats that sailed these waters and someone was sure to come.

Finally a ship, rather far out, dropped anchor and sent out a skiff with two sailors to bring us in. It was a large vessel, carrying cargo that had been loaded in Panama. Freight had been sent to the isthmus, on the other side, then transferred to the Pacific side by rail and loaded into another ship for delivery in California. Despite all the traveling and transferring, Captain Forker told me it was still less expensive to ship cargo this route than overland. It was cheaper to bring carpets, furniture, pianos, and so on, and safer.

It was a fine ship and the captain was kind, but they were bound north, and I had to get to the south somehow. Captain Forker explained my situation to Captain James, who finally said, "Well, it would be best to put the boy ashore again and let him walk south to the nearest village; there he could probably pick up a fishing smack to carry him around to La Paz."

"How far might the next village be?" I asked.

Captain James studied his map and calculated. He said he thought there was a small fishing settlement about twenty miles south.

"Oh, I could walk that!" I exclaimed.

I had been looking over Captain James's shoulder at the map and I saw that the long isthmus of Baja California was very narrow.

"Couldn't I make it cross-country to La Paz?" I asked. "It doesn't look to be so far."

"I doubt it. It's dry country and hilly, too. I wouldn't know about water. And it's Indian country. They might not be friendly. No, better make for a fishing village."

In the end, Captain Forker came to shore with me in the skiff and gave me a big hug for goodbye. He gave me money and said he would pray that all went well.

"I hate to leave you here, Güero. Maybe you better change your mind, come on back north with me and get a boat in San Diego to take you at least as far as Cabo San Lucas."

"I'm afraid it would take too long. And it would cost so much!"

I watched Captain Forker row back to the ship, and then I saw it get under way and begin the voyage north.

I started south. It was lonely, but I was not frightened. El Coyote and Brazo Fuerte had taught me to feel at home in the country, and to look on all the creatures of the countryside as possible friends. Even the rattlesnake always gave warning, and one could get out of his way.

I continued walking most of the day, except for a short

rest under a tree when the sun was highest, to wait out the worst heat. As I lay dozing, I became conscious of someone near, someone I couldn't see. I looked all around, but I couldn't discover anyone, or even any grass or bushes moving. Yet I felt myself observed.

When darkness began to fall, I wondered about a place to sleep. The trees were short and scrubby, windblown and leaning toward the east.

I sat down on a rock near some bushes and drank a little water and ate some of my cold meat and crackers—a gift from Captain James. Suddenly a shape materialized. It was an Indian, dressed in skins. At first he said nothing, made no sign to me, but I had a feeling he meant no harm. I made a motion to offer him water and food, and then he came forward slowly.

He made gestures toward his chest and then imitated rocking a baby. Suddenly it was clear to me; he was one of the Indians who had come to my mother when she and Padre José had baptized so many infants.

He accepted food and drank sparingly from my water bottle.

I waited to see what he wanted. I thought he must want something, because he had shown himself and tried to communicate. When full dark came down and the stars began to glitter in the sky, he rose from where he had been crouching and motioned to me to follow.

I went with him and we walked through the night for several hours. Then, far ahead, I saw a glimmering light, and as we came nearer, I smelled roasting meat. He was taking me to a village.

Though it was dark, I guessed we had been walking east, and I wished to go south, but I decided it was prudent to fall in with his plan, so I bowed and made gestures of peace toward everyone, as we came into the village. My companion had instantly silenced the dogs, and he called out in a language I didn't understand. I was brought meat and then taken to a strange sort of tent made of skins, very low and small, but inside it was warm, out of the wind and cold. I lay down and slept soundly.

In the morning, they gave me food again, and took me a little distance away where a spring was bubbling slowly out of the earth, ending in a tiny stream. I drank and filled my water bottle. The Indian who had led me, and seemed to be in charge of me, filled a large water pouch made of skins, shouldered it, and then made motions to me to follow. He gestured toward the north, and it came to me that he planned to take me back home.

I shook my head, and finding a firm place in the earth where I could write with a sharp stick, I tried to make him understand that I wished to go south. Then it occurred to me that maybe he could guide me over the mountains to La Paz. I drew a map, showing the end of the peninsula, and I made motions around it, and drew a line up toward where I had indicated a small bay. Then I drew a line directly across from the bay, La Paz, to where we were. I did this several times, pointing to my chest and showing that I wished to go there. He seemed not to understand, and I despaired. I sat down and hid my head in my arms. He stood up then and left me swiftly, and I did not see him for some time, perhaps an hour.

Meanwhile, I tried hard to remember the few Indian words El Coyote and Brazo Fuerte had taught me.

When he came back, and squatted beside me, I tried my words on him. But he still did not understand.

Then he took the stick that I had been using to make the map in the earth, and drew something wavy. I took it he meant mountains, and he spread wide his arms, to show great size, and then he shook his head sadly.

So he had understood me, after all. He started north, but I refused to follow and he came back. Then he sat, and seemed to be lost in thought.

Once more he took the stick and showed me where we could go north some way, then east, and pass over to the other side. He did this several times. I was delighted. He was telling me we must go north to reach a pass and that then we could drop down on the Sea of Cortés side.

I took the stick and followed his line and then, making him look at me, I made the line follow down to La Paz, along the sea on the other side. I placed my hand on my chest and then on his, to show that I would follow him. He smiled and stood up, and looked at the sun.

From the village he collected some food, acorns and dried meat, and we started out. He was a fast walker; he leaned forward and went at a little trot. I had no choice but to try to imitate him or get left behind. I got into the rhythm and was able to follow, but I tired and had to sit down after a few miles. He motioned to a little clump of trees ahead, and continued at his fast trot, and I went, limping along behind. When we got to the shade I lay down full-length. He gave a sort of grunt, which I had come to recognize as assent.

He let me sleep until the sun had slipped down the sky and shadows were lengthening. Then we shared some of the water and food, and started out again.

My companion tried to tell me his name. He pointed to himself and grunted something that sounded like Quat. I told him to call me Güero, but he could not say it. He just shook his head and said some word that I supposed meant "Boy."

We traveled for eight days. I kept a stout branch as a sort of cane, which could be used as a club if needed, and I made notches in it for each day that we walked.

I noticed that our supply of acorns was gone, and that Quat shared out the jerky in increasingly smaller portions. Then he made me sit in the shade under some bushes, to wait for him, and he took my club with him. He was gone several hours. But toward dusk he returned carrying two squirrels, which he skinned and gutted, and after we made a fire, we roasted them and had a good supper.

He was very kind to me. I appreciated his careful search for safe places to sleep, his care over me while I slept, for often I woke to find him sitting up, alert and watchful, and he always made calming motions toward me, and covered me with one of his coyote skins.

Then came a day when we were climbing steadily all the day, progressing upward along riverbeds and animal paths; we came to a sort of peak, and prepared to start down on the other side. Looking out, I saw the distant blue ribbon of the sea.

From this height we dropped down swiftly toward the strip of land that bordered the Sea of Cortés. We found fishing villages, where we were well treated and given plenty to eat. Then we marched south, and passing other small villages, at last we came to where there was a large settlement; instead of tents and huts, there were large buildings around a lovely sheltered bay. Boats were anchored in the bay, and I knew it must be La Paz, at last.

Quat stopped, and pointing with his right hand, he then gave me a little push. He wanted me to go on alone. I tried to thank him, but he didn't want me to touch him or hug him. I tried by gestures, every way I could think of, to show my appreciation, my affection. But he made no sign and his face did not change expression; he just pushed me again.

So I went forward. After about a quarter of a mile, I turned and looked back, and waved. He was still there, watching me. He did not wave back, but lifted his right hand, held it high for a moment, and then turned and started away at his fast trot.

8

La Paz was not really much of a town. Just barracks and houses made of mud bricks. But there were a fair number of them. The town was busy and there were many soldiers about. I stopped one and asked the way to the office of the comandante.

The soldier looked at me and laughed. Then he spit and made motions which were rough and very clear. He meant for me to go away.

"I am a Mexican citizen," I shouted, "and I have to see the comandante."

"Get out of here, dirty Indito" was the answer.

My ruined clothes, my coyote skin, my bare feet, my rough hair made him think me an Indian. Even my fair hair and green eyes did not deceive him, for I heard him jesting with another soldier.

"Look at that blond Indian boy! Our soldiers get around, eh? Mixed blood there! Get along, Indito. Go to the village; they will give you something to eat." He pointed to a straggle of tents and a few adobe lean-tos, covered over with branches.

I tried other soldiers, but I was pushed away, sometimes roughly. In desperation, when night fell, I did go over to the Indian village and I held out my hand for something to eat. In silence I was given a bone, with some shreds of meat on it. A few young boys tried to talk to me, but I did not know their language, nor they Spanish. I was allowed to sleep under a shelter, where some Indian youths lay. The place seemed to be a sort of dormitory for young boys, because other Indian youths came and lay down, and an old woman peeked in now and then, as if to make sure we were all right.

In the morning, it occurred to me to go down to the shore and see if I could find a sailor who might help me. The boats rocked out on the bay, and nobody seemed about to row in to shore. But I could not give up. I settled down to wait.

I was rewarded. Late in the afternoon, a dinghy holding about six men was launched from the largest of the ships and rowed toward shore. I was in the water when they beached, wading out to them, and I was determined to make somebody listen to me.

To the man who stood up and seemed to be an officer, I cried out, "Sir, I must speak to you! I hold an Amparo from my father, Judge Cayetano Treviño!"

The man, who was in fact the comandante of the town, with authority over all of Baja California, sat down heavily in the dinghy, surprised. He looked astounded.

"I am not an Indian!" I shouted. "I am Porfirio Treviño. I am a Mexican citizen! I have walked all the way from Ensenada. I have an Amparo which you must respect!"

This was not true. I had not walked all the way, only partway, and I did not have the Amparo. But I had to get his attention.

To my joy, the comandante listened to me. Leaping out onto the dry sand, he took my arm and looked into my face, studying it.

"You are not an Indito," he said.

"I am the son of Judge Cayetano Treviño. He is held prisoner in the jail in Ensenada by Captain Alanis, but my father has written an Amparo. Only the soldiers won't let him out of jail and they tore up his Amparo! You must send soldiers to fight them and set my father free!"

"Come with me, *hijo*," he said, and my hopes rose, for he had called me son.

He took me with him to his office, in one of the best buildings in the town. It was of adobe, like all the others, but quite spacious, and there was good Mexican furniture in the rooms; there was a rich rug on the floor, there were curtains at the windows, and the comandante took his seat behind a fine desk.

He called an orderly and commanded, "Take notes. This is important."

Then he turned to me and said, "Tell me everything, *hijo*. Speak slowly and carefully. Do not forget anything. You speak good Spanish; you come from a cultured home.

You have been educated. Begin with your father. What is he doing in Ensenada?"

I told him the whole story, and I did not leave out the filibuster Jack Morris, the adventurers from the north who were moving into Mexico's territory, taking up land without titles, exploiting Mexico's mines. Finally I told about my father being thrown into the little jail and how Brazo Fuerte had got the Amparo out, and the long tube, and the crack in the adobe wall. And I told how Don David Zárate, who had shown the Amparo to Captain Alanis, had also been thrown into jail. And lastly I told him all my troubles and how I had finally been able to get to him, at La Paz.

When I finished and fell silent, he sat quietly for some time, thinking things over. Then he called the orderly again. "Get this young man some clothes and a place where he can bathe."

To me, he said, "I shall give orders to make the boats ready and we will sail for Ensenada as soon as possible."

The orderly did as he was told, though the clothes he brought me were all too big. He had put together a wardrobe from the clothes of the smallest soldiers at the post. The sleeves and trousers had to be rolled up and straw stuffed into the boots, but how wonderful it was to wash with soap and put on clean clothes! They even cut my hair, which had grown long around my ears and in back. I could hardly wait to get started on the journey home on the same ship with the comandante. Oh, how I longed to see my father's face again, to know him free and triumphant, instead of enduring humiliation and ill-treatment.

But I had to wait two days.

Meanwhile, I ate well in the soldiers' mess, and slept deeply, and kept my clothes clean.

At last we were ready and I followed the comandante onto his flagship, with high hopes.

Many times during that voyage, the comandante spoke to me and asked me many more questions about Ensenada and everything that had happened.

"It is our own fault, that is, Mexico's," he said sadly. "We have not yet definitely agreed on our northern boundaries, and we have not defended them properly, as a sovereign state should. Naturally, adventurers from everywhere will take advantage. We must be good neighbors with the people in northern California, what we call Alta California, and we can be so only when we know and respect each other's rights, and defend them. It is when we do not know what to expect of each other that there is trouble.

"Your father, the Judge, is right and I will uphold him. Land titles, water and mining rights, the requirements for emigrating and settling, all these things are regulated by law and must be respected. I am bringing a surveyor, who will get busy and lay out the center of the town, and lines going out from it, so land titles can be marked and proved. There is much to do."

"What will you do with Captain Alanis?" I asked, hoping to hear that he would punish him severely.

"I will do nothing," he answered sternly. "He will be taken away and tried by a military court, and they will pass sentence. I will simply relieve him of his post and send him to La Paz and later to Mexico City."

With that, I had to be content.

Sometimes the comandante spoke to me about his family, far away in Mexico City, and I began to remember our own house there, and the stables and horses and carriages, and the school and all that my life had been. How far away it seemed!

"My wife stayed behind with our son when I was ordered to La Paz," the comandante told me, "because he is very delicate and could not stand the journey or the life in Baja California, where we lack so many things that make life easy and comfortable. My son had a severe fever when he was five years old and it left him crippled in the legs. He will never be able to be a soldier like me."

"Perhaps he will be a judge like my father," I said, and this seemed to please him, because he put his arm around me and gave me a hug.

We rounded Cabo San Lucas that same day and began our journey north along the coast. It was a beautiful voyage. The sea was calm, rolling gently, and a deep blue. The coast was almost always in sight, brown and golden, with the dark purplish hills in the background. Each day succeeded another like beads on a chain. Everyone was good to me. But I was nearly mad with eagerness to get home, to see my father and mother and our friends. And I wanted to see Captain Alanis marched away with soldiers in front and in back, as he had made my father march.

But when the moment actually came, it was very swift, and though I was overwhelmingly happy to see Papacito and Don David come out of the jail, and to embrace them, I could not rejoice as much as I had planned, seeing Captain Alanis marched away to disgrace and perhaps prison himself. He looked so devastated, it was like watching something die.

We had a wonderful reunion and feast at our house that day. Everyone joined in and Tía Vicky and Mamacita sang all day and cooked rabbit and vegetables and fish, and sent dish after dish to the trestle table that had been set up under the oak tree. Mamacita would stop singing and laugh and cry all at once, and hug Papacito again, and then look at the cooking. I guess Tía Vicky really did most of the work. Brazo Fuerte had come back, and El Coyote was there, too.

I told them about the Indian who had guided me and taken care of me, and Brazo Fuerte said, "Yes. I sent word."

"How could you do that?" I asked. "And how could you know what had happened when we were practically shipwrecked?"

"We have ways. You were watched all the way down the coast, from when Captain Forker docked here to where you had to beach the boat. And then we sent a friend to guide you."

"Then, Brazo Fuerte, I need not have gone at all. You could have done it."

"Oh no. They would never listen to me."

"That's true. They wouldn't listen to me either, when they thought I was an Indian."

His face did not change, but I knew I had hurt his feelings, and I was sorry.

"When I am big, and a judge like Papacito, I shall change all that and you and your people shall sit in the high councils and be judges, too!" I cried. Then I knew he felt better and I was forgiven.

Afterward, Papacito had his court again and a clerk and helpers, and Don David brought lumber from Oregon and built fine houses for many of us, and the town began. The titles were given out and registered, and the name of our place was El Ciprés, named for the row of cypress trees down near the beach.

We were very happy and I thought that our wonderful life would go on forever. El Coyote and Brazo Fuerte and I studied with Tía Vicky and we were free afternoons to make our gardens, or go hunting or fishing, or just climb around the hills and explore.

But then Don David came to visit us, as he was planning another trip north to the United States.

"Don Cayetano," he said to Papacito, "we must think about educating our boys."

Instead of answering at once that Tía Vicky was educating us very well, my father looked thoughtful and pulled at his beard.

"You are right," he finally said. "Where do you think we should send them? To Mexico City?"

"No. To the United States" was the answer. "There are good schools there, and it is reasonably near. They could come home on vacation. You see, Judge, they must learn English. Our country will always be dealing with the Americans, especially we men from Baja California, and our boys must know the language and know it well."

Papacito was thoughtful a few days and he and Mamacita talked together quietly and stopped whenever I came near. And Mamacita seized me and hugged me very tight every now and then.

Then one evening they asked me to stay after supper, and the three, Papacito, Mamacita, and Tía Vicky, told me it had been decided that I was to go to school in San Diego. We would go on Captain Forker's boat, renamed the *Emily II*, Tía Vicky and I. She would stay to buy me clothes and get me started in school, and she would choose supplies to bring home. I was to stay all year, but they promised I could come home in the summer.

"Until . . . ?" I asked, unhappy.

"Until you are eighteen, and then you must go down to Mexico City, to enter the university."

This seemed a long time. Too long. I did not look forward to it. At least, I thought, Coyote will be with me.

"Coyote will be going to the same school, won't he?"

"No. His father is taking him farther north, to a big school in Santa Ana. You will have to make new friends, Güero, and learn new ways. We thought it better to separate you, for if you were together you would speak Spanish all the time, and the important thing is to learn English."

There was great excitement getting ready and waiting for Captain Forker. Coyote and his father left on the stagecoach, which came more often lately.

I had said goodbye to everyone, and was climbing up on the *Emily II* when I began to feel very sad. I waved and waved, until we were far out on the water and the figures of Papacito and Mamacita and Brazo Fuerte grew small and then disappeared.

Then, as we moved away, everything was a blur of blue water, brown land, and dark hills, and it was just as if my life had never been. Gone were my family, my friends, the garden I had planted and watered, the cypress trees, and the shore and rocks I knew. It would never be the same, because I would never be the same.

"Well, Güero," said Captain Forker, dropping his arm around my shoulders, "you'll be beginning a new life. You'll have good experiences and bad ones. That's what life is. But you'll enjoy it, that I promise you!"

"And you can do anything, Güero," cried Tía Vicky. "You have proved that!"

I supposed they were all right, my parents, Tía Vicky, Captain Forker, all of them. I had to go forward, I had to learn. I had to get ready for the rest of my life.

We were standing at the rail, looking back. When Tía Vicky turned and went toward the companionway that led to the lower deck and our cabins, I turned, too, and followed her.

The new life was already beginning.

AUTHOR'S NOTE

The Güero of this story was my father-in-law, Ing. (Civil Engineer) Porfirio Treviño Arreola. He told me about his adventurous boyhood in many short snatches, when he had time, or when he recalled some special incident. He remembered countless details of his early years on the long, hard journey from Mexico City to Ensenada, and he always spoke with undying affection of his friends in Baja California.

I have put together the story, as I could piece it out, adding some invented characters and incidents in order to tie it all together and form a continuing narrative. Those parts of the story I devised, but, on the whole, El Güero's exciting life was a true adventure. He lived every moment of it, and he never forgot it.

I was present when the two old friends, Güero and El Coyote, met again, after fifty years. They were so moved that they clasped each other in a hug, and both wept.

There was a Brazo Fuerte. There was a little sister Maruca, who had diphtheria, and the Judge tried to save her life by performing a tracheotomy himself. There were filibusters, and land swindles, and Judge Cayetano Treviño was thrown into jail without trial. Brazo Fuerte did secretly get the Amparo out. And El Coyote had indeed been car-ried away by an Indian nurse and lived as an Indian some years of his boyhood.

When at last I made a journey to Ensenada, where much of the story took place, I was able to meet a son of El Coyote's, who told me that Indians had often come to speak to his father in their own Indian language, which he never forgot.

A distant relative of El Güero, Don Hesiquio Treviño, lives in Ensenada and is an authority on the history of the region. To him I owe much help and excellent advice.

The ranch called El Ciprés, where El Güero lived, is now a military barracks, but it is still known as El Ciprés.

To Don David Zárate, El Coyote's son, and to Don Hesiquio, I beg pardon for any errors I may have made, in the hope that they will forgive me for any details that are inaccurate. Every word I wrote was based on my father-in-law's loving memories, and my deep respect.

I loved my father-in-law, Ing. Treviño (El Güero), very much, and in telling of his courageous boyhood, I honor his memory, and with it, the memories of all the friends he loved.

Elizabeth B. de Treviño